WINNING PLAYERS TALK ABOUT BASKETBALL, FAMILY, AND FAITH

DAVE BRANON

Editor, *Sports Spectrum*

MOODY PRESS
CHICAGO

PHOTO CREDITS:

Cover: David Robinson slam dunks over the Los Angeles Lakers on his way to the 1999 NBA championship. Photo courtesy of Allsport USA/Todd Warshaw.

Calbert Cheaney, Hubert Davis, LaPhonso Ellis, and Bryant Stith photos © NBA Properties, Inc. Used by permission.

Todd Fuller photo courtesy of Robert Walker

Brian Skinner photo courtesy of Brian Skinner

All other player photographs courtesy of the Boston Celtics, Charlotte Hornets, Chicago Bulls, Houston Rockets, Milwaukee Bucks, New York Kickerbockers, and San Antonio Spurs clubs of the National Basketball Association.

ISBN: 0-8024-7929-4

To the chaplains in the NBA, who are making a difference in the world of sports by influencing the athletes in the league to put their faith in Christ, especially to Bruce McDonald of the Philadelphia 76ers; Mike Rohrbach, formerly of the Seattle Sonics; Chip Bernhard of the Milwaukee Bucks; and Claude Terry, who oversees the chaplaincy program through Pro Basketball Fellowship.

To my family, for whom I write and without whom nothing this valuable and important would be worth doing.

Contents

Acknowledgments

Anybody who knows a trey from a layup knows basketball is a team game that must be won by a concerted effort. One person, even if he is Michael Jordan, can't do it all.

Putting together a book such as this also takes a team effort. It cannot be done without the thankless cooperation of a large number of people. Here's a look at the team members who cooperated to make this book possible.

Washington Wizard Calbert Cheaney gave of his time to be interviewed at the 1998 Jammin' Against the Darkness crusade in Washington, D.C.

Jan Drew, the wife of Valparaiso coach Homer Drew and father of Bryce, was most gracious when I called to set up the interview with the Rockets' first-round draft pick.

Another family member who was helpful was Jennifer Hawkins, who made sure her husband, Hersey, who suffers as most men do with "I hate to return phone calls" syndrome, got in touch with me. Also, thanks to the Hawkins' good friend, Bruce McDonald, who encouraged our contact. Bruce is the chaplain for the 76ers.

In Denver, assistance came from Jerry Schemmel, the voice of the Nuggets, and Tommy Shepherd, the team media relations person, as I lined up interviews with Bryant Stith.

For most players, it was their agents or their agents' assistants who cleared the way for interviews. In that regard, Joel Bell had the best batting average. I asked him for help with three of his clients: Hawkins, Andrew DeClercq, and Brian Skinner. He came through with all three.

Likewise, Steve Kaufman, Hubert Davis's agent, was extremely cooperative. In the midst of trying to take care of megastar Scottie Pippen, agent Jimmy Sexton came through in my request to speak with Elliot Perry. And Herb Rudoy assisted my contacts with Andrew Lang, who made good on a promise he had given me personally two months earlier to do the interview.

Tracy Hartman, who does the contact work for Tom McLaughlin, LaPhonso Ellis's agent, was very thorough in her work. It was a similar situation for Ann Stewart from the office of Richard Howell, Brent Price's agent. Both delivered their men.

As did Jocelyn at Terre Williams Agency, a group that helps Charlie Ward find good outlets for his story.

Robert Walker of US Sports is always willing to help, as he did with my request to speak with Todd Fuller.

Others who helped included Christin Ditchfield, one of my top *Sports Spectrum* writers, who generously helped with David Robinson.

Resources used to provide supplemental information for this book included the following: *Sports Spectrum* magazine, *Sports Spectrum* radio, *The Sporting News NBA Guide, The Sporting News NBA Register,* NBA media guides, *ESPN Sports Almanac,* and *Slam Dunk.*

Foreword

When I think of NBA basketball players, like many fans I marvel at their athletic gifts, their conditioning and skill levels, their competitive spirit, their popularity, their incomes, and even their lifestyles. For four to five nights a week these are some of the things on public display. And if not on display, then certainly these are the things most written and talked about when it comes to NBA players. However, if your perspective is shaped only by what's on the surface, you'll be misled.

The NBA is not without warts. The 1998–99 lockout served as the most recent image-wrecker, not to mention off-court troubles for at least one owner, plus several players and officials. The league has plenty of work to do to rebuild a more positive image, and I think it will.

As a former player, and now as a TV commentator for the Indiana Pacers, I've been fortunate to be around the game and the players for the last eighteen years. In that time I've seen the league grow dramatically in popularity and size. The league also has gotten younger and less polished and more physical and defensive in its style of play. There have been many other changes across the NBA landscape, but suffice it to say, change is inevitable. Some changes are good and some aren't. I'd like to focus on one of the positive changes as it relates to the players.

Upon entering the NBA as a player back in 1982 with the Indiana Pacers, I really had no spiritual foundation in my life. I was a decent guy, but I lacked a personal relationship with God through faith in Jesus Christ. But through a combination of people, circumstances, and the fledgling NBA chapel program, in 1986 I discovered God's plan for my life through the Bible and God's Son, Jesus Christ.

At that time there were only twenty-three teams in the NBA, and maybe half had chapels. Today there are twenty-nine teams in the NBA and just about all have chapels. Across the league, players, coaches, management, and media personnel attend chapel where the Word of God is proclaimed boldly and clearly. Many NBA players are devout Christians who through their testimonies and lifestyles are bearing witness to the glory and goodness of God. In attitude and service toward their teammates and communities, many NBAers are allowing their lights to shine, thus having an impact on others for eternity.

Some of those players are the ones you'll read about in this book, while others are unknown to you now but are in the process of being planted and watered in the faith. God is at work in and around the NBA, working in the hearts of many to will and to act according to His good pleasure.

CLARK KELLOGG
TV Analyst
Indiana Pacers and CBS Sports

Introduction
Beyond the Dollars

When I first began working on this book, I was making more money than every professional athlete I interviewed. That's not because I'm some flush author who drives around in a Miata while the Land Rover's in the shop. No, I was making more money than all the guys I interviewed because none of them were getting paid.

I conducted most of the interviews during the NBA lockout, which led in 1999 to the shortened 50-game season. That marked the last time in world history that a writer who works for a Christian ministry made more than a professional basketball player.

In fact, some of the young men I talked to had not even received one cent of money from the teams that drafted them. Guys like Brian Skinner and Bryce Drew were still trying to get in shape for training camp without the benefit of the financial rewards from being first-round draft picks.

Of course, now that the lockout is history and everyone is again getting paid to play, the rest of us can go back to trying to figure out how many lifetimes it would take for us to earn what Shaquille O'Neal makes for hitting a free throw.

The thing that struck me about this whole concept of money and the NBA is that I could sense little difference in guys who were making lots of money back in 1994, when I interviewed them for *Slam Dunk,* and the guys who were making no money when I talked to them for *Slam Dunk 2*. Well, there was one thing. I think I noted more humility and more spiritual maturity in the players this time around than I had noticed a few years ago.

In the truest sense, this book is not about the money. Sure, it is sometimes hard for us to not grow a bit jealous of the huge paychecks pro basketball players receive. But when you get a chance to talk with them, you realize that money doesn't change anything. And, in fact, money doesn't run their lives.

They are still humans with the same need to be needed, the same need to have a God to serve, and the same need to nurture their relationship with Him.

For me, the players became real in a variety of ways. There was my conversation with Jennifer Hawkins, who knew that her husband, Hersey, was a typical man who didn't like to return phone calls. Or my phone call to Hubert Davis just as he brought home some new dogs and had to keep an eye on them so they "won't tear up the house." Or the call to Todd Fuller, who was a great interview despite his bad cold. Or LaPhonso Ellis, whose contagious laugh and obvious pleasant spirit were a real joy.

These were not people who relished the fact that in 1999 their league was squabbling over millions of dollars. They were just nice people who happen to play a high-profile sport and are constantly in the public eye.

I genuinely liked these men for their candor, their dedication to Jesus Christ, and their obvious gratitude that God has given them the opportunity to play professional basketball. Now that they are back to making big money, I don't begrudge them their perks at all.

My desire is that you find them spiritually encouraging as you read about their struggles and their joy in serving the Lord.

Calbert Cheaney
The Heart of a Hoosier

VITAL STATISTICS

Calbert Nathaniel Cheaney
Born: July 17, 1971, in Evansville, Indiana
6 feet 7, 215 pounds
College: Indiana University
Position: Guard/Forward
Family: Single

CAREER HONORS

- Led all NBA shooting guards in field-goal percentage, 50.5% (1996–97)
- Only Wizard to start in all 82 games (1997–98)
- Two consecutive 30-point games as NBA rookie (1994)
- Division I College Player of the Year (1993)
- First-team All-American (1993)
- Wooden Award and Naismith Award winner (1993)

NOT-SO-VITAL STUFF

- Eats spaghetti for his pregame meal
- Loves the Dallas Cowboys and the St. Louis Cardinals
- Has worn number 40 since the fourth grade

FAVORITE VERSE

"For God so loved the world that he gave his one and only Son, that whoever believes in him shall not perish but have eternal life" (John 3:16).

Calbert Cheaney

You can take the boy out of Indiana, but you can't take Indiana out of the boy.

That seems to be the case with Calbert Cheaney. Cheaney, who has been one of the bright spots in a rather frightening past few seasons for the Washington Wizards, will never seem like a man of the city. He may have moved to D.C. with his outstanding basketball skills, and he may light up the MCI Center with his presence, but he'll always be a Hoosier at heart.

Who but a true Hoosier, for instance, would be so effusive in his praise of one sometimes controversial, and often inflammatory, red-sweatered coach named Bob Knight? Calbert Cheaney, who at one time thought he blew his opportunity to play basketball for Coach Knight and who in the beginning would rather have gone to Purdue to play for Gene Keady, has only good things to say about the Bloomington Bomb.

Let's go back to Calbert's hometown of Evansville and follow his climb to stardom.

Before he would ever get to a point at which Knight would be interested in him, Cheaney had to pass through several stages in his basketball life. It all started for the somewhat shy Calbert when he was in elementary school and his teacher, Mr. Curcio, casually asked Calbert, "Have you ever played basketball before?"

He really hadn't—at least not on a team—but that question and his subsequent interest got him started on the road to superstardom. Calbert was nine years old. "I took to it," he says now in an extreme understatement. "God's given me some nice abilities, so I was able to take to it really well. It just took off from there."

As young Calbert continued to play, he may have taken to the sport, but he admits that he didn't demonstrate any tendencies toward stardom for quite a while. "As far as athletic ability, I was ahead of most kids. But in terms of basketball ability, I wasn't really that good. My basketball ability had to catch up with my athleticism. It really didn't catch up until I got to high school, and then not until my junior year."

Cheaney was, he admits, just "one of the guys" for the first half of his high school career.

That would all begin to change, though, when an astute varsity coach, Gerald VanDevinger, pulled him aside and in effect gave him permission to move his game up several notches. At the time, Cheaney was a sophomore on the junior varsity team.

"Calbert, you have a great ability," VanDevinger told the youngster in his office. "You have a chance to play Division I basketball in college. If you just work hard, you already have the athleticism. You could become a great basketball player."

Whether it was this little speech or Cheaney's maturity as a basketball player that made the difference, no one can ever really know. But something happened, because Calbert went from being a good JV player to a hotly contested major college recruit within a matter of months. The fact that today he credits his coach with spurring him on to greater things is a real testament to the power and the inspiration of a good high school coach.

Calbert worked on his game during the summer by participating in the Amateur Athletic Union (AAU), traveling to summer tournaments all around the country. His AAU performances attracted the attention of coaches from schools across the country. The University of Southern California was the first to show an interest in the budding star. But as this self-described "late bloomer" blossomed, along came the others: Purdue, Indiana, and Kentucky.

Purdue was Calbert's first choice, followed by the Kentucky Wildcats. Then Indiana. But Indiana liked him a lot. When Calbert was a junior at Harrison High School in Evansville, the ultimate compliment was paid to him: Coach Bob Knight traveled to Harrison High to see Cheaney play. But the player wasn't impressive.

"I stunk up the gym," Calbert says with candor. "I shot something like 8 for 25. I only had 17 points, I wasn't very aggressive, and our team got beat at home. I think Coach Knight left at halftime."

Cheaney figured it was all over for his chances at Indiana, although at the time that wasn't much of a problem since his heart was set on Purdue, the "other" Indiana school in West Lafayette. "I figured he didn't take me seriously. He must have thought, 'He's not gonna be that great of a player.'"

Knight never came back to see Calbert play in high school. But he wasn't through recruiting him. Ron Feldman, one of Knight's assistants, did return to see Calbert play.

Cheaney had a great summer of AAU play between his junior and senior years, and his senior season was stellar. Feldman continued to follow Cheaney, eventually reporting back to Knight that Calbert was "by far the best player out of all the recruits." Finally, Coach Knight, who "trusts his assistants," according to Cheaney, said, "Let's go get him."

But first, Calbert had to sort through the fact that he really preferred Purdue and Kentucky.

"I liked Kentucky, where Eddie Sutton was coaching." But before Calbert got too serious about playing in Lexington, the Wildcat program ran into some trouble with the NCAA. That knocked Kentucky off his list. As for Purdue, Calbert had a campus visit but discovered once he got there that he "just didn't like it."

When he visited Indiana University, though, he discovered that "it was great. Plus, it was only two hours from home."

As things worked out, it seemed to be the right place for Calbert Cheaney. Shy by nature but incredibly focused while on the basketball court, Cheaney was able to withstand the inevitable Bob Knight onslaught.

It would seem that one of his major challenges would have been to tolerate and withstand Knight's outbursts of crude language. Cheaney, who trusted Jesus Christ as Savior when he was twelve years old and who was a regular at Greater St. James Missionary Baptist Church while growing up in Evansville, could easily have struggled with such treatment. He was, however, able to tune out the negative to receive the positive instruction Knight offers—just as other Christian stars at Indiana before him, such as Kent Benson and Steve Alford, had done.

"You've just got to let it go in one ear and out the other," Cheaney says. "And you just have to keep your faith in God and the abilities He has given you so you can play the game. You've got to recognize that that's just how Coach Knight is. He's a very disciplined coach, and if you do something wrong, he's gonna let you know about it. It might not be the words you want to hear, but I learned to block it out. I didn't always listen to what he said, but why he said it.

"If you're going to play for him, you have to have a strong attitude. But he'll push you to the NBA and beyond."

Cheaney didn't just play for Bob Knight; he became a bona fide star for him. During his junior year, he helped the team get into the NCAA Final Four. But when he was a senior, Cheaney became a rare commodity indeed. He averaged 22 points a game on the way to becoming the college basketball Player of the Year, taking home the Naismith Award and the John Wooden Award, an honor that includes not just basketball skills but academic prowess as well. In his senior year, the Hoosiers made it to the Elite Eight in the NCAA tournament.

For the kid who didn't impress Knight just a few years before, it was a dream year. "It was a great experience," he says. "We had a great team, a bunch of great guys. I'm just glad the Lord blessed me with having a good season that year. When I went into the season, I didn't think I was going to blossom like I blossomed. I think a lot of it is because I had faith in God. I think that my confidence in the ability He gave me carried me through. That year might have been one of the greatest times of my life in terms of basketball. I wouldn't trade it for anything."

With the end of his career as a Hoosier, it came time for him to leave the comforts of Indiana for the challenges of the nation's capital. Taken by the Washington Bullets with the sixth pick of the first round in the 1993 draft, Cheaney was expected by many to become a star in the league.

During Cheaney's rookie year in the NBA, most of his playing time came in a substitute role, playing behind Rex Chapman. But when Chapman went down with an injury, Cheaney started 21 games, averaging 15.8 points a game during that stretch. In two games in February 1994, he showed how much he belonged in the league when he racked up back-to-back 30-point games. Against Minnesota he knocked down 30 and the next game he went for 31 against the New Jersey Nets. Seven times during his rookie season, Calbert led the Bullets in scoring.

Cheaney's best year in the scoring column came in his second season, 1994–95, when in 78 games he scored 1,293 points to average 16.6 points for the campaign. In addition, he had his best season for assists, with 177, and his second best year in the steals category, with 80.

When the Bullets (renamed the Wizards before the 1997–98 season) acquired Chris Webber, some of the pressure was off Cheaney to score as much, for Webber regularly averages 20-plus points a game. In fact, the trio of Webber, Juwan Howard, and Cheaney combined to average 62 points a game during the 1995–96 season (23.7; 22.1; 15.1).

Throughout his career with Washington, Cheaney's stats have been tied not necessarily to his skills, which have never been questioned or diminished, but to his teammates. During the final years Webber was with the team, there were periodic episodes of negative behavior—both with Webber and his former Michigan teammate Howard. Cheaney could have succumbed to the negative situations that surrounded him on the team. There were times when his teammates seemed ready to self-destruct through their sometimes questionable activities. For Cheaney, though, it has not been too difficult to overlook those problems and concentrate on his job.

"You've just got to have faith in God and continue to play hard. A lot of people make mistakes. The players on our team are great guys. I love them to death."

One of the reasons Cheaney could stay strong was the influence during his first five years of Joel Freeman, team chaplain. Although Freeman left that position before the 1999 season, Cheaney gives him a lot of credit for his own spiritual growth. "Joel is a real man of God. He stepped up and did whatever he could to help us. He reaches out to us and we reach out to him so he can help us gain more of a knowledge of Christ. I really admire him for doing that."

Those years of personal growth and the guidance of Freeman lead Cheaney to become involved in 1998 in two activities that showed his desire for men, women, boys, and girls to know Jesus Christ as Savior.

The first action is also another indication that although Cheaney lives in the Washington, D.C. area, his heart is still back in Indiana. In August 1998, Cheaney traveled back home to help dedicate the Greater St. James Missionary Christian Education and Recreation Center. And his help included his wallet: Calbert donated $630,000 so the church could build this outreach center.

"There aren't a lot of things kids can do," Cheaney says of the Evansville neighborhood where he grew up. "There's not much to do except hang out on the street, hang out on the corner, drinking brews and all that other stuff. Deal in drugs. That kind of thing.

"I wanted to build a recreational center right next to the church, right in the ghetto to keep kids off the streets. It gives them an opportunity to have fun but also to learn about God, and that's the main issue."

When the church first set out to do something for the kids, Pastor Douglas F. Smith had no grand ideas of building such a structure. At first, he was going to use some new property the church had purchased and put up some outdoor basketball courts. When Pastor Smith told Calbert of those plans, the Wizard forward said, "Why just stop there? Why don't we build a recreational center?" Then he told his pastor, "God has blessed me with the financial ability, so let's try and build a rec center."

That center now has a full-size gymnasium, a multipurpose room, volleyball courts, a dining area with a kitchen, and a children's playground. While the center operates as an outreach for young people, the church hopes someday to offer day care, senior citizen activities, and teen pregnancy counseling.

About a month after the center was dedicated in Evansville, Calbert was back in the nation's capital playing basketball at the MCI Center, the Wizards' home court. But not for the NBA, of course. Remember this was 1998, a year in which no NBA teams played any basketball anywhere after the NBA finals ended in June. It was the year of the lockout.

So, what was Cheaney doing in D.C.?

He was participating in another activity that showed his heart for those who need to know Jesus Christ as Savior. He was in his home arena to help several other NBA players and an evangelist as they brought the gospel to some 18,000 people.

The event was called Jammin' Against the Darkness, and its goal was to use the fame of NBA players to draw fans to an arena where the players could share with the crowd the importance of faith in Jesus Christ. Joining Calbert in this September activity were A. C. Green and Hubert Davis of the Dallas Mavericks; Hersey Hawkins of the Seattle Sonics; Andrew Lang of the Milwaukee Bucks; David Wood, journeyman NBA player; and Darrell Green of the Washington Redskins of the NFL.

After an opening round of basketball games played by the NBA stars (some three-on-three, some three-point shooting, some two-ball), the players one-by-one took the microphone and shared their faith with the people in the nearly full arena.

When it came time for Calbert to speak, he turned from a rather reserved star to a well-spoken cheerleader.

"Are you having fun yet?!?!" he entreated the assembled.

When the response didn't meet with his expectations—how often does an NBA star get to judge his expectations of a crowd rather than the other way around?—he yelled, "I can't hear you!!" That, of course, resulted in a much louder and much more satisfying response from the throng.

Then Calbert told them, "Repeat after me: 'God!'"

The crowd screamed, "God."

"Is!"

A loud "Is" followed.

"Good!"

The gathering echoed Calbert's words.

Imagine getting 18,000 people, many of whom know nothing about matters of faith, to say in unison, "God is good."

Then Cheaney stood in the middle of the court, near the spot where he usually nails an occasional three-pointer, and told the story of his salvation back home in Evansville.

Then he said, "If you don't know what to do with yourself, trust Jesus. Tonight, put all pride aside. God gives you a choice: to accept Jesus as Savior or not. I'm not going to mess around. I want you to be on our team. That's what it's all about."

Finally, in a move that was designed to ensure that everyone in those cushioned seats knew the gospel, Calbert had everyone stand and repeat John 3:16 after his lead.

As the night continued, the remaining players gave their testimonies. Later, after special guest artists dc Talk had brought their own style of praise to the arena, it was time for evangelist Steve Jamison to present the gospel in unmistakable terms. At the end of his message, hundreds and hundreds of people came from all over the arena to the front of the stage placed at one end of the basketball court. There they were met by counselors, who prayed with them if they were coming to trust Christ as Savior.

It was a remarkable evening.

Why did Calbert Cheaney put his faith on the line in front of people who in a few months would be coming back to watch him play NBA basketball? One reason was the aforementioned Joel Freeman. "He asked me if I wanted to do this," Calbert says. "I jumped at the chance because it gives me an opportunity to help some souls be saved."

The young man from Indiana had done what he could to help Evansville with the building of a rec center, and now he realized his new hometown needed help as well. "This city [D.C.] is one of the top murder capitals in the world. A lot of stuff goes on and a lot of people might spite God because they don't know Him. People will say, 'There are people getting killed here every night. Why is it happening?' We just have to try to go out there and help the people who do not know Him."

It's obvious that Calbert Cheaney has a heart for people that helps him carry on in a league that sometimes offers things that Christians must ignore and turn away from.

Whether it's the influence of an ungodly teammate or the outside influences of some of the nasty sideshows of NBA hangers-on, it can be a difficult life for a believer. Cheaney, though, has the ability to work with all kinds of people and still stay strong.

"I really don't think it's that tough," he says of life in a league with a relatively few Christians. "I'm friends with a lot of guys in the league, and they may not have the same views I have. I've never witnessed having people not like me for the way I carry myself. I just have to keep my faith in God."

Calbert has gone a long way and he's gone a lot of places in his basketball travels. But he keeps coming back to what he discovered as a twelve-year-old in Evansville. For Calbert, home is where the heart is.

Q & A WITH CALBERT CHEANEY

Q: *How did you feel speaking out at the Jammin' Against the Darkness?*
Calbert: I was really nervous. I didn't know what to expect, but I was excited. David Wood and Andrew Lang told me how it was and not to be nervous. They told me to play to the crowd and at the same time help them learn more about Jesus Christ.

Q: *What helps you grow spiritually?*
Calbert: Studying the Bible. I don't read it as much as I should, but it helps me. Every time I study the Bible, I call my mom and she helps me understand what I read. I need to start reading it more instead of watching TV.

Q: *You seem to respect Bob Knight for his loyalty. Talk about that.*
Calbert: When it's all said and done, when you graduate, he'll do anything for you. That's the type of person he is. He'll go through anything that you have to go through in terms of getting a job. If you're hurt or something is wrong, he's willing to listen. If you've played for him, you'll always be a member of the team.

NBA ROAD

1993: Selected by the Washington Bullets with the sixth pick of the first round of the NBA Draft. The Bullets changed their name to the Wizards before the 1997–98 season.

THE CHEANEY FILE

Collegiate Record
College: Indiana University

Season	Team	G	FGM	FGA	Pct.	FTM	FTA	Pct.	Reb.	Ast.	Points	Avg.
89–90	Ind	29	199	348	.572	72	96	.750	133	48	495	17.1
90–91	Ind	34	289	485	.596	113	141	.801	188	47	734	21.6
91–92	Ind	34	227	435	.522	112	140	.800	166	48	599	17.6
92–93	Ind	35	303	552	.549	132	166	.795	223	84	785	22.4
Totals		**132**	**1018**	**1820**	**.559**	**429**	**543**	**.790**	**710**	**227**	**2613**	**19.8**

Three-point field goals: 1989–90: 25-51 (.490); 1990–91: 43-91 (.473); 1991–92: 33-86 (.384); 1992–93: 47-110 (.427). **Totals:** 148-338 (.438).

NBA Record (Regular Season)

Season	Team	G	FGM	FGA	Pct.	FTM	FTA	Pct.	Reb.	Ast.	Points	Avg.
93–94	Wash	65	327	696	.470	124	161	.770	190	126	779	12.0
94–95	Wash	78	512	1129	.454	173	213	.812	321	177	1293	16.6
95–96	Wash	70	426	905	.471	151	214	.706	239	154	1055	15.1
96–97	Wash	79	369	730	.505	95	137	.693	268	114	837	10.6
97–98	Wash	82	448	981	.457	139	215	.647	324	173	1050	12.8
1999	Wash	50	172	415	.414	33	67	.493	140	75	385	7.7
Totals		**424**	**2254**	**4856**	**.464**	**715**	**1007**	**.710**	**1038**	**1483**	**5399**	**12.7**

Three-point field goals: 1993–94: 1-23 (.043); 1994–95: 96-283 (.339); 1995–96: 52-154 (.338); 1996–97: 4-30 (.133); 1997–98: 15-53 (.283); 1999: 8-37 (.216). **Totals:** 176-580 (.303).

Hubert Davis
Bad Things into Good

VITAL STATISTICS

Hubert Ira Davis Jr.
Born: May 17,1970, in Winston-Salem, North Carolina
6 feet 5, 183 pounds
College: University of North Carolina
Position: Guard
Family: Single

CAREER HONORS

- Finished fourth in NBA in three-point shooting, 43.9% (1998)
- Finished third in NBA in three-point shooting, 47.6% (1996)
- Only New York Knick to play in all 82 games (1994–95)
- Led ACC in three-point shooting, 48.9% (1991)

NOT-SO-VITAL STUFF

- His mother is part Cherokee Native American
- His uncle, Walter Davis, played in the NBA
- Bought two dogs during the last week of the 1998–99 lockout

FAVORITE VERSE

"And whatever you do, whether in word or deed, do it all in the name of the Lord Jesus, giving thanks to God the Father through him" (Colossians 3:17).

Hubert Davis

ame the top three men's college basketball coaches of the last part of the twentieth century. Coaches who through their sheer genius and their outstanding records as mentors of players are seen as the best in the game. Coaches who are noted for their keen insight into the ability of guys and who are known for being able to get those outstanding players and mold them into a championship team.

Probably one of those coaches you named was Dean Smith, the longtime head man at the University of North Carolina. Smith's credentials are impeccable and his laurels are virtually endless. Even before he was through coaching, the arena where his team played was named after him. He has sent dozens of players to the NBA. His name is mentioned in the same sentences as men such as John Wooden.

But he's not perfect.

In fact, sharpshooting pro basketball player Hubert Davis once told Coach Smith, "You're no judge of talent."

Now, before you get the wrong idea about the veteran guard from the state of Virginia who has turned shooting three-pointers into an art form—after his first six years in the NBA he was the third-ranked trey-shooter in league history—understand this: Hubert made that comment to Coach Smith purely in jest.

Yet there is one sense in which what Hubert said is accurate.

Hubert Davis was a star athlete at Lake Braddock Secondary School in Virginia, especially in football and basketball. He received his talent honestly. His dad, Hubert Ira Davis Sr. was, as Junior says, "a tremendous basketball player." Plus, his uncle, Walter Davis, played in the NBA for fourteen years, twice making the All-NBA second team and capturing the 1977–78 Rookie of the Year Award with the Phoenix Suns. Davis Sr. averaged 24 points a game in his first year in the league.

So when Hubert Davis began to show that he was a star athlete, he began to garner the attention of football and basketball coaches. In football, teams such as Syracuse, West Virginia, and Virginia all sought out Hubert's services as a wide receiver. In basketball, he was picked as one of the Top 100 high school players in the land. Hoops coaches began to trickle into Lake Braddock to observe Hubert. They came from Virginia and Indiana. And North Carolina.

The North Carolina thing, Hubert admits, probably scared away a few other recruiters. He made no secret that he wanted to go to Chapel Hill to play for the Tar Heels. "I think everyone knew I wanted to go to North Carolina," he says. "They all knew that if I had a chance at all of going to North Carolina, I was gone. I think schools like Duke just said, 'Forget him.'"

There was a small problem with this plan. And it had to do with the venerable Coach Smith.

"Coach Smith came to see me play, and I did well," Hubert says of his visit from the dean of coaches. But apparently he didn't play well enough, for Smith had a surprise for Hubert.

"He told me not to come to North Carolina," Hubert says. "He said he thought I wasn't good enough to play at UNC. He said I should go to a lower Division I school to guarantee playing time. He didn't think he would be able to give it to me."

This was not an easy thing for Dean Smith to say to Hubert Davis, because Smith had coached his Uncle Walter at North Carolina. "He had known me for so long, and he felt bad," Davis says of Smith.

Yet, as a favor to Hubert because of Walter, Coach Smith

decided to give the youngster a scholarship. He also told Hubert that the scholarship did not ensure any playing time. He would have to earn his spot on the team.

"He had it in his mind," Hubert says, "that for four years I would be a benchwarmer. I had to not only play well but also to show him that 'Look, I should be playing.' It was really tough."

So Hubert went to North Carolina on a mission. And he accomplished it.

While a member of the Tar Heels, he accumulated some outstanding statistics and honors:

- Fifteenth all-time in scoring (1,615 points)
- Eighth-best all-time free-throw percentage (.819)
- Second all-time in three-pointers (197)
- 21 points per game average as a senior
- Scored 35 points against Duke in one game as a senior

As a junior, Davis helped usher the Tar Heels into the Final Four. "That was something I had always dreamed of playing in as a little kid. To finally get there, and for it to be a far greater experience than you could even imagine, was awesome."

Davis and his Tar Heel teammates made it to the last round of the NCAA playoffs in 1991. During the regular season, North Carolina was 25–5. Along the way, they beat Northeastern, Villanova, Eastern Michigan, and Temple to earn a trip to the Hoosier Dome (now the RCA Dome). There the Tar Heels played the 12th-ranked Kansas Jayhawks, losing to Roy Williams's team 79–73.

To Davis, that still stands out as his most memorable basketball moment—even outdistancing playing in the final game of the 1993–94 NBA Finals as the Knicks took on the Houston Rockets in a losing cause. "That was intense," he recalls of the NBA title game. "But playing in front of . . . 50,000 people in the RCA Dome was incredible."

So, yes indeed, Hubert Davis proved to Dean Smith that he could play Division I basketball at the highest level. And he still gets a kick out of reminding his old coach of that fact.

Smith, as anyone who knows anything about him is aware, keeps close tabs on his former players, talking to them "almost every week," Davis says. And it's not a favoritism situation. According to Hubert, "Not only does he talk to me every week, he talks to the walk-ons who graduated. He talks the same way with the walk-ons as he does Michael Jordan [who left North Carolina in 1984 to pursue NBA superstardom]."

So, now, when Smith and Davis get on the phone, the NBA star has a little fun with the retired coach. "I always tell him, 'You're no judge of talent.' And he goes [Hubert now assumes his best high-pitched imitation of Dean Smith's voice], 'You're right. You're right.'"

Clearly, between the time he was a star high school player trying to get into his favorite university and the time he graduated from UNC, much changed for Hubert Davis. And Hubert would agree his life changed forever when he was sixteen years old. That's when what he jokingly calls his "Brady Bunch" family was devastated with the most horrendous of tragedies.

When he was sixteen, Hubert's mother died of oral cancer.

"We had just a great atmosphere in our home. It was a loving home." And he had a special closeness with his mother.

"She was very beautiful," Hubert says of his mom. "You know how you have a close connection with one of the parents. In our family, it was my dad and my little sister, Keesha. And my mom and I had the same personality. We were extremely close. My mom was a Christian, and she always talked about God. She took me to Sunday school and church, but I had no interest in that."

For a young man who already was not predisposed to having loving thoughts toward God, the death of his mother made the gulf between the two even greater. "When my mom died," Hubert says, "I hated God. I could not understand. Everyone said, 'It's God's purpose.' I was like, 'Well, then, He's a terrible God.' I struggled with why God would take away such a great person when there are so many bad people in the world. She was the last person I thought should leave this earth. It was very tough for me."

That's how things stood between Hubert and God for the

next few years. As he made his mark in high school sports, as he left for college, and as he battled his way to stardom at the University of North Carolina, Davis harbored this hatred toward God in his heart.

Nothing changed until the summer before his junior year at Chapel Hill.

That's when the friendship of some Christians on campus began to pay off. "When I went to college, a lot of people who got to know me, and some of my friends, saw the struggles I was going through, and they were Christians.

"They said to me, 'Hey, why don't you go to church with us. Maybe you can find some answers.'

"So I went to church every Sunday. And I went to prayer meetings, just trying to find out why my mom went. As I kept going, I started to realize that I needed a change in my life. I began to see how much God loved me."

As Hubert's heart began to grow softer toward the truths of God, an Athletes in Action campus leader, Mike Echstenkamper, approached him after church. Hubert recalls, "Mike came up to me and said, 'You need to talk, don't you?'

"I was like, 'What?' Then I said, 'Oh, yeah, I do.'

"We started talking, and talked for hours and hours. That was Monday, and by Wednesday I had become a Christian. That was the best thing that ever happened to me," Hubert says.

Before giving his life to Christ, Hubert had been transferring all of his hostilities and his efforts into basketball. Without some outlet for the feelings he had concerning his mom, he turned his heart solely toward the sport he loved. "I took life too seriously," he recalls. "And I used to take basketball too seriously. If I shot poorly, I was in a terrible depression."

That changed when Hubert trusted Christ. "Basketball is still extremely important to me. But it's not everything."

The change affected other areas of his life as well. "Reading the Bible taught me how I needed to live my life—even in terms of how to treat young women. It helped me recognize that I could be a good influence on people by the way I play basketball.

"And it helped me with my mother. I didn't hate God anymore. I don't think I'll ever find the answer to my question, 'Why?' I don't think I'm supposed to know. The only thing I can say is that I'm glad I had her for sixteen years. I know that I'm going to see her again some day. That's the good part."

But what about Hubert's dad? Before, Hubert would go to Mom when Dad was too hard on him. What now? Well, their relationship has gotten better and better. "When my mom died, we really had to bond. Now we have a unique father-son relationship." While Davis moves around the country playing in the NBA, Hubert Sr., who works for the U.S. Department of Education in Washington, D.C., keeps in touch through frequent phone calls. In 1998, Keesha graduated from college. It's not been an easy road since Hubert and Keesha's mom died, but the family has stuck together and kept going.

Another thing that has kept going is Hubert's basketball career. On the strength of his high-scoring career at North Carolina, and especially his senior year, in which he scored 21 points a game, Davis set himself up to be drafted by the NBA.

Yet as the day came for the draft, Hubert was not absolutely sure he was going to get that coveted NBA opportunity. The experience of current NBA veteran and former UNC teammate Scott Williams gave Hubert cause to wonder about his future.

"My sophomore year, Scott Williams, who was a great player, was supposed to be picked, and he wasn't." For the record, the 6-foot-10 Williams averaged 14 points and 7 rebounds a game for the Tar Heels in 1989–90. And although he was not drafted, he eventually signed as a free agent with the Bulls in 1990 and collected a couple of NBA championship rings.

But it was Williams's draft snub that worried Hubert. "I knew that sometimes you just get passed over for some reason. So I was a little nervous during draft day. There were teams that drafted before New York, and when they didn't pick me, I was thinking, 'Oh, no! They don't want me.'

"I'd call my dad and say, 'I'm never going to get picked.'

"He'd say, 'Don't worry. It's OK. I think you're going to get picked soon.' My dad always has the ability to make me feel better. After I talked with him, I was OK."

Finally, while the selection process was still in the first round, Hubert Davis was picked by the New York Knicks. He was the 20th selection of the first round.

From the beginning of his NBA career, Davis has been depended on by the teams for whom he played to produce long-range shooting. Some players can reveal their secrets to launching the three-point bomb by talking about technique or practice or some fine point of skill. For Hubert, though, the reason for his success from downtown is as much a mystery to him as it is to the people he shoots over.

"I have no idea why I can shoot the three," he says. "I don't spend any more time on that than I do on any other part of my game. It's nothing I concentrate on and try to make a part of my game. It just happens. For some reason, I've been able to shoot out there. All I can say is that it's God's strength. In high school, I only shot four threes. I couldn't shoot them at all. But over the years, I've just gotten stronger."

Hubert contends, though, that the three-point shot is not all his game is about. "I don't think I'm just a three-point shooter. . . . Because I shoot them well, people think that's all I do. I just love the game. It doesn't matter what I'm doing. Defense. Passing. Rebounding. I love to win."

When Davis's career began, he was with a team that not only loved to win, but was good at it. In his first year with the Knicks, the men from Gotham won 60 games during the regular season and battled Chicago six games before losing the Eastern Conference Finals.

The next season was even better. Pat Riley's men won 57 regular season games and went all the way to the NBA Finals before losing to the Rockets in seven games. That year Davis became a force, becoming the Knicks' fourth-leading scorer.

The next two seasons, the team won another 102 regular season games. For someone who wanted to win, it was the right place to be. And it seemed that the feelings were mutual. During the 1995–96 season, Knicks' general manager Ernie Grunfield said, "We'd like to keep Hubert as a Knick for his whole career." Those must have been words of deep pride and comfort to Davis at the time.

That summer those words rang as hollow as a bouncing basketball in an empty Madison Square Garden. On July 24, 1996, the Knicks sent Hubert packing to the Toronto Raptors. After four years, a .449 shooting percentage on three-pointers, and 2,492 points, Davis was traded north for a 1997 draft pick.

"When I got traded to Toronto," Hubert says, "that was my lowest point in basketball. It was nothing against the Toronto Raptors' organization. It was just the first time I had ever been traded. It was a tough experience. It was really tough to swallow the fact that the Knicks didn't want me. To go to another team changed my life.

"The only thing that got me through it was God. It was hard going from a championship caliber team to one that lost 52 games. It was really difficult. It took away everything I was used to."

Davis was injured twice that year, missing three and one-half months of a six-month season. "God took away everything that was comfortable to me," Hubert admits. "Basketball. The winning and all that stuff. He let me realize that He's the most important thing in my life. It refocused me to make me realize that I wasn't here to play basketball. I was here to serve God. Even though it was a downtime in my career, it was the best thing that could have happened to me."

Hubert Davis, it seems, has learned over and over in his life to let the worst thing become the best thing.

His mother dies, and he hates God: It eventually leads him to a saving knowledge of Jesus.

His dream of playing for North Carolina is interrupted by a legendary coach who doesn't think he's good enough: He works so hard that he becomes a star.

His comfortable role with the perennial playoff-team is ripped away from him: He calls it a good thing because of the lessons it taught him.

Besides, that trade to Toronto in the summer of 1996 would lead to what Hubert calls the best career move of his NBA saga. On September 4, 1997, he signed a free-agent contract to play for the Dallas Mavericks.

That could be viewed by many as a step down from the

Toronto Raptors. After all, the Raptors won 30 games in 1997–98 while the Mavericks won just 24. So, for a man who had won at every level from college through his first four years as a pro, how could this be good?

"When I was a free agent, I wondered, 'Maybe this team, maybe that team.' Dallas never entered my mind at first. It's just awesome how when you let God work in your life, He'll put you in a place where He thinks it's perfect for you, not where you think is perfect. I never thought Dallas would be the place, but it's been the best place.

"The city is great. The people are tremendous. But it's the teammates that make it best. To have A. C. Green on the team is great. And just to be part of a team where I like to be with the guys is a blessing. I haven't had that since college."

The NBA road for Hubert Davis may or may not end in Dallas, but it seems to be his understanding that God can put him wherever He wants and it will turn out for the best. He has developed an attitude that allows him to roll with the changing scene of NBA life without allowing it to throw him off.

But, of course, that's what faith can do. And since Hubert is a man who is serious about keeping his faith strong, it seems that no matter where he goes or what team he suits up for, he'll find it to be the best situation. That's a man who has learned to trust God no matter what.

Q & A WITH HUBERT DAVIS

Q: *What is something you've done recently that has helped you grow spiritually?*
Hubert: During the lockout, I tried fasting from TV for a week. I go to [Dallas pastor] Tony Evans's church, and he challenged us to fast from food or something that we really do a lot. Something that would take away from spending time with the Lord. So for one week, I didn't watch any TV, which is huge for me. It was very hard, but it was very good for me. It taught me that I don't need to watch all these TV channels, and it's given me time to get a lot of stuff done. But most important, it's given me an opportunity just to relax and spend some time with the Lord.

I didn't have to feel like, "OK, I've got to watch this TV show." When you do that, you shortchange your prayers and your reading time. That was the first time I have ever fasted in any way, so it was pretty cool.

Q: *What is something NBA fans don't know about the NBA but should know?*
Hubert: That there are some nice guys. I think media reports and news in general are so negative. I wish they would do more positive stuff. There are many people in the league who work hard, who take pride in their jobs, who are just solid Christians and solid citizens. Unfortunately, all the media reports on is when we get in trouble.

Q: *What steps do you take to keep yourself pure in the sometimes immoral world we live in?*
Hubert: You need to be honest about it. If you put yourself in a tempting situation, probably nine times out of ten you're going to muff it. The key is to put yourself in situations where you won't fall. I'm not going to go out on a date with someone and not tell her about me, which is, how much I love God.

NBA ROAD

1992: Selected by the New York Knicks in the first round of the draft

July 24, 1996: Traded to the Toronto Raptors

September 7, 1997: Signed by the Dallas Mavericks as a free agent

THE DAVIS FILE

Collegiate Record

College: University of North Carolina

Season	Team	G	FGM	FGA	Pct.	FTM	FTA	Pct.	Reb.	Ast.	Points	Avg.
88–89	NC	35	44	86	.512	24	31	.774	27	9	116	3.3
89–90	NC	34	111	249	.446	59	74	.797	60	52	325	9.6
90–91	NC	35	161	309	.521	81	97	.835	85	66	467	13.3
91–92	NC	33	241	474	.508	140	169	.828	76	52	707	21.4
Totals		**137**	**557**	**1118**	**.498**	**304**	**371**	**.819**	**248**	**179**	**1615**	**11.8**

Three-point field goals: 1988–89: 4-13 (.308); 1989–90: 44-111 (.396); 1990–91: 64-131 (.489); 1991–92: 85-198 (.429). **Totals:** 197-453 (.435).

NBA Record (Regular Season)

Season	Team	G	FGM	FGA	Pct.	FTM	FTA	Pct.	Reb.	Ast.	Points	Avg.
92–93	NY	50	110	251	.438	43	54	.796	56	83	269	5.4
93–94	NY	56	238	505	.471	85	103	.825	67	165	614	11.0
94–95	NY	82	296	617	.480	97	120	.808	80	150	820	10.0
95–96	NY	74	275	566	.486	112	129	.868	88	103	789	10.7
96–97	TOR	36	74	184	.402	17	23	.739	40	34	181	5.0
97–98	DAL	81	350	767	.456	97	116	.836	135	157	898	11.1
1999	DAL	50	174	397	.438	44	50	.880	85	90	457	9.1
Totals		**429**	**1517**	**3287**	**.462**	**499**	**595**	**.832**	**651**	**781**	**4028**	**9.4**

Three-point field goals: 1992–93: 6-19 (.316); 1993–94: 53-132 (.402); 1994–95: 131-288 (.455); 1995–96: 127-267 (.467); 1996–97: 16-70 (.229); 1997–98: 101-230 (.439); 1999: 65-144 (.451). **Totals:** 499-1150 (.434).

Andrew DeClercq
No Laughing Matter

VITAL STATISTICS

Andrew Donald DeClercq
Born: February 1, 1973, in Detroit, Michigan
6 feet 10, 230 pounds
College: University of Florida
Position: Forward/Center
Family: Single

CAREER HONORS

- Finished third on team in rebounds, 4.8 (1997–98)
- Recorded first double-double (10 points, 10 rebounds) on April 10 (1996–97)
- Set a school record by starting all 128 games during college (1995)
- Selected All-SEC first team (1995)
- Played in the Goodwill Games in Russia (1994)

NOT-SO-VITAL STUFF

- Still roots for boyhood favorites, the Detroit Lions and the Tigers
- Collects model ships and other items related to the sea
- Nickname is "Drew"

FAVORITE VERSE

"'Love the Lord your God with all your heart and with all your soul and with all your mind.' This is the first and greatest commandment" (Matthew 22:37–38).

Andrew DeClercq

You've got to like a guy who laughed when his college coach told him he thought he was good enough to play in the NBA.

There are many things about Andrew DeClercq that are not typical of the NBA players fans have grown accustomed to these days. But perhaps the most endearing aspect of his life is the fact that he finds it surprising that he is making a living as a basketball player.

Aren't we more accustomed to players who started swaggering around the junior high gym when they were thirteen with an "I'm destined for the Big Show" attitude? By contrast, there is Andrew DeClercq, who actually narrowed down his college choices by finding out which school had the best program to train him to become a civil engineer. He says of his early college days, "I was going to school to get an education. And then when college was done, I would look at getting a job."

Imagine that. A bruising 6-foot-10 rebounder thinking about working for a living!

It's really no surprise, since basketball and other sports weren't the end-all and be-all for young Andrew DeClercq as he was growing up. Oh, he established some fan-type ties with the Detroit Tigers, Pistons, and Lions when he and his parents and sisters lived in Detroit. And he played a little baseball and some basketball and even more soccer. But his parents never really pushed him into sports, and he contends that he wasn't all that crazy about them.

"I never really liked basketball or baseball that much," he says. "Soccer was probably my first love."

As a freshman at Countryside High School in Clearwater, Florida, he was still playing and loving soccer. That changed, though, during his first year of high school "when I hit a growth spurt of about five inches in about three months."

Andrew had always been tall ("I was always the tallest kid in my class," he says), but suddenly he was basketball tall. The freshman explosion put him at 6 feet 7 or 8 and made it pretty much mandatory that he'd be moving from the soccer pitch to the gym.

That doesn't mean he was an exceptional basketball player at this point, though. "My freshman year, kids would just laugh at me because I would trip over the lines on the court. Going through that growth spurt was difficult. There was some awkwardness."

And to make matters worse, Andrew was shy. He really didn't mind being tall, exactly. In fact, his goal had always been to be as tall as his 6-foot-6 dad, a milestone he passed that freshman year.

"I was never uncomfortable with being tall. My awkwardness came because I was shy. When I would go out in public, everyone would notice me. For a shy kid, being noticed is not what you want. I wanted other people to just accept the fact that I was tall and say, 'He's just another kid.'"

After this awkward stage during his freshman year, though, things began to improve. He began to get serious about getting better on the court by going to summer basketball camps. "Once I grew out of my clumsiness, it became more fun. I started liking basketball."

Something that happened during his sophomore year increased the enjoyment even more. He began the basketball season on the junior varsity team, but when a couple of the big players on the varsity got hurt, Andrew was moved up. Supposedly, this was done simply to assure a full complement of players at practice. But when it came game time, the coach realized he needed this youngster to fill in during competition.

"The plan was for me to go back to JV after Christmas," Andrew says, "but I was doing so well at that level that they didn't think it would be worth it to send me back. So they just left me up on the varsity."

Good move, coach.

A year later, it was not just his high school coach who was noticing Andrew. Major college coaches began to let him know they were watching. "People started talking about college scholarships," Andrew recalls, still expressing amazement. "I thought, 'Oh, wow! I could go to college for free and play basketball. Cool.'"

Cool indeed. Keeping in mind that he wanted a school that could educate him for the workaday job he figured he would need after college, Andrew narrowed his choices down to Duke, Virginia, and Florida. They all had the kind of architecture and engineering instructional paths he was looking for.

At the time, there was a clear distinction among those three that had little to do with the classroom. Duke and Virginia, he knew, were basketball schools. Florida was not.

"Duke and Virginia were ACC [Atlantic Coast Conference] schools," he explains. "If you wanted to play basketball, that's where championships were coming from. If I went to Duke or Virginia, they probably would have redshirted me. They were also recruiting guys like Alan Henderson, Glenn Robinson, and Cherokee Parks [all now in the NBA]. I was fifth or sixth down the line on their wish list. They told me that. They were honest with me, and I thanked them for that."

No overinflated pride or soaring ego got in DeClercq's way. He knew where he stood, and he knew that he was not suited to battle the competition for playing time at a basketball factory.

So he considered Florida. "I knew that going into Florida, I was going to be able to play right away." Early in his senior year, then, he signed a letter of intent to become a Gator.

As DeClercq headed into his final year at Countryside, though, an obstacle sprang up to put doubts in his mind about his college career. "I had just signed with Florida when I broke my elbow. I had a screw put in my elbow, and it took a long time to heal." He couldn't practice for three months, and he began to have doubts: *Will I be able to bounce back stronger? Will I have a full range of motion?*

During that summer, after graduating, he traveled up to Gainesville to work out with some Florida players and discovered he was fully healed. He was able to play hard and play well. He was ready for his first year of college.

Physically, that is. Spiritually, he was somewhat like he had been back in his high school freshman year on the basketball court: clumsy and not ready for the big time.

When Andrew was eight years old, he had trusted Jesus Christ as his Savior. His mom, who had taken him to church his whole life, sat down and explained the gospel to him. Although he realizes now that he didn't understand very much, he knew that he needed to be saved, and he was.

But for the next ten years or so, while he was growing taller physically, he was pretty much remaining undersized spiritually. "I was not able to understand everything God wanted for me for my life. I kind of accepted Christ and said, 'There. I'm saved. I'm a Christian,' and left it at that."

It wasn't that Andrew became a drug-pushing drunkard with a pack of cigarettes rolled up in his sleeve. It was more a matter of not growing—of depending on outward appearances instead of growth from the heart. "I just kept thinking, 'You're a good kid. You follow the rules. You don't cuss. You don't drink. You don't have sex, and you'll be fine.'" In effect, Andrew was a Christian with his life in neutral.

That would change, though, after he had spent some time at the University of Florida. First, he came under the direction of Dave Stelling of Campus Crusade for Christ. He helped light a fire under the big guy.

"He opened up a lot of new worlds. He'd have me read some books and do a lot of Bible study. We had a lot of discussion times. I learned that my faith was more than just a decision I made when I was eight. I began to see that it is a relationship between Jesus and me. I found out that there is so much more out there that God can give us. So many blessings. The way I had been living was so shallow."

During a summer Athletes in Action camp Andrew attended in Colorado, he finally came to grips with what he needed to do. As Stelling explains, "Being around other Christian athletes, he began to see how God is interested in every area of his life."

While this was going on spiritually for DeClercq, some great things were also happening in the basketball area, beginning with the relationship with one of his new teammates, Dan Cross. The two were roommates during Andrew's first two seasons.

"We talked a lot about the team, [asking each other,] 'What are we going to do to get this team to the next level? What do we need to do to get there? What sacrifices would we have to make?' We put in a lot of time working on our games and learning what we had to know."

Early on, DeClercq showed that he had the stuff to lead the Gators to new horizons. In his first year, he started every game, led conference freshmen in rebounding, made the SEC All-Freshman team, and set the tone for his teammates with his all-out, nonstop, high-energy way of playing basketball. In both games and practice, DeClercq was noted for his intensity. It was not uncommon to see his 6-foot-10 frame sprawled all over the practice floor after he had dived for a loose ball. As a sophomore, the improvement continued. This time, he made the All-SEC second team.

At the end of his sophomore season, Andrew sat down for the watershed conference with coach Lon Kruger, the one that made Andrew laugh at the incredible notion that he could possibly play in the National Basketball Association.

It was the typical, end-of-the-year, here's-what-you-should-work-on-this-summer talk with Coach Kruger. "We always had really candid talks," Andrew recalls. "They told us where we were, what we had to work on, and what we had to improve on. Coach Kruger sat me down and said, 'You can play in the NBA.'"

When he saw the amused look on Andrew's startled face,

Kruger continued. "Don't laugh. I'm serious. You're 6-10; you're 220 now. I can see you at 240. The way you run the floor, the way you rebound, there will be NBA teams that would love to have you on their team. You need to think like that. If that's where you want to go, you need to think in those terms."

For the first time, as a twenty-year-old, soon-to-be college junior, Andrew DeClercq began to see that his future might include wearing an NBA logo, complete with a silouhette of Jerry West, on his uniform.

And he got serious.

"I kind of shifted my priorities away from school, and I put more of my efforts into basketball. I still wanted my degree, but I changed my major."

His current track at that time—civil engineering—took him on a five-year journey to graduation, and he knew he didn't want to stay that extra year if he was going to pursue pro hoop dreams. So he changed his major to history.

"I hadn't taken a history course since high school," he says.

One thing he knew about history, though, was that he, Dan Cross, and their teammates wanted to make some of their own at Florida. And that's just what they did during Andrew's junior year.

They won and won and won. Twenty-nine times they came out on top. Their 29–8 mark in 1994 was a school record number of victories. And the Gators made it to the Final Four, which Andrew calls "the biggest moment in basketball for me." In the semifinal game at the Charlotte Coliseum, the Gators fell 70–65 to Duke—the school where DeClercq was sure he wouldn't get much of a chance to play.

By now, it was a foregone conclusion that DeClercq would get his shot at the NBA. And for the first time, it seems, he was letting it take over who he was. "I hit a bit of a dry spell spiritually toward the end of my senior year," Andrew admits. "I started rebelling a little bit. I never went out and said, 'I'm against God.' It was just that I put Him on the back burner."

This continued through the time he was drafted and into his first couple of years with Golden State. He was a professional basketball player now, but in a spiritual lethargy. That changed during the 1997–98 season when, as a Boston Celtic, he got a spiritual wake-up call from Bill Alexson, the Celtics chaplain.

"A lot of it was realizing that the way I'd been living was not right," DeClercq says of his spiritual renewal. "I began to realize that if I was going to call myself a Christian, I needed to start acting like it a lot more. Alexson brought me back to what I should be living for and what my priorities should be . . . putting God first."

That adjustment in his spiritual life opened up new avenues for DeClercq when he entered the long, lonely world of the 1998 lockout of NBA players. He still considers the lockout one of the toughest things he has had to go through.

"It was difficult trying to figure out what is best for the sport, what's best for the players now, and what is best for the players who are going to be coming up. And I had to consider what is best for me individually. It's tough, because you listen to the fans, and they were pretty upset about it. They were sick of it.

"I read a comment one day that really struck home. A guy said, 'Let's see what you get when you make money your god.' It shocked me a little bit and made me sit back and think. It was just one line, but it's a very strong statement. When I looked at it from my background and my beliefs, I knew it was very true. It made me do some soul-searching. 'Why am I really doing this? Why am I here? Where is my life going?'"

Part of that answer came for DeClercq during the lockout when he began to get much more involved in his church in Clearwater. He began to be active in the youth department, helping teach the kids. As the lockout came to an end and he had to report to training camp, he was thinking of picking up one of the Sunday school classes to teach.

And he was learning from the leaders in the church. "The pastor really challenges us every day to go forth and multiply and reach others with the gospel. The church is centered on outreach, on loving God, and on bringing new people. Being involved in that has bolstered me to want to do more.

"I've learned that being a Christian is not a Sunday thing. It is who you are. Our church is tremendous for challenging us to follow the commands God has given us." Those were spiritual adjustments DeClercq was willing to make as he continued on his NBA path.

Adjustment was also the key word for Andrew DeClercq physically as he made his way through his first three years in the NBA.

As a second-round draft pick by the Warriors in 1995, he knew he was not one of those players who are thrust into the starting lineup and allowed to learn on the job. It was a struggle to earn playing time.

"I understood that it was another step up to be in the NBA. But until you get into the game and see how good some of those guys are—how big and strong they are—you never truly understand. Everyone was the star of their team in college. And when you first start in the league, they're all older and more experienced."

Each year, DeClercq moved another step closer to that older, more experienced category. As a rookie with Golden State, he played in just 22 games. The next year, he played in 71 games, scored 357 points and grabbed 298 rebounds. And he showed flashes of brilliance, with games of 17 points and 15 rebounds, good stats in any league.

"In college, there are games when you are in control. You're in a zone. You see things happening a little slower. You move to the right spot, and the ball bounces to you instead of away. You feel energized. There have been a handful of games like that in the NBA. It's getting to the point where I'm very comfortable with what I'm supposed to be doing."

With Boston in the 1997–98 season, DeClercq did something he had done at Florida: He played in every game. That gave him the opportunity to get more comfortable and to post bigger stats: 439 points and 392 rebounds. Then, during the lockout-shortened 1999 season, he showed his continuing maturity. Moving from Boston to the Cleveland Cavaliers, he averaged 7.9 points per game, his highest NBA points average.

In a sense, Andrew DeClercq proves that there is no typical NBA player. While we might think the players in the league all dreamed of being the next big star as kids, DeClercq's experience shows that this is not always true. While we might think the players don't consider thoughtfully their roles and the relative significance of the money they make, DeClercq's contemplations during the lockout prove that some players do.

But most important, his somewhat up-and-down struggle with living for Jesus proves that even though things look mighty glamorous and easy for NBA players, they all face struggles. They all need to come to grips with who they are before God. Thanks to a caring college mentor, a wise NBA chaplain, and a challenging pastor, DeClercq seems on his way to becoming a solid Christian example who can continue to teach us many valuable lessons about life in and out of the NBA.

He's not laughing anymore about his NBA prospects. He knows he has a serious position now as a role model, teacher, and teammate.

Q & A WITH ANDREW DECLERCQ

Q: *What is something you don't like about the NBA?*
Andrew: Everything outside the lines—the lifestyle. It takes a lot to stay away from some of the bad stuff that's out there. There are a lot of guys who I would say are Christians who have fallen by the wayside and have gotten their priorities messed up. They know the truth. They grew up in the church. They accepted Christ. They believe. But then they get sidetracked.

It's tough because so many players get put on pedestals. It's tough to fight off, to keep your humility. And it's very easy when you've got everyone telling you, "You're the greatest." You can begin to think, I make all this money, I can do whatever I want. I can get in trouble and I might get a slap on the wrist.

Q: *Why is Matthew 22:37–38 your favorite Bible passage?*
Andrew: [To love the Lord with all your heart, soul, and mind]—there is so much in there. Our purpose is to love God. Everything else is secondary.

Q: *What is something you like to do to stay strong spiritually?*
Andrew: I like to listen to tapes. I also do a lot of reading because we have time on airplane rides and in hotels between games. I've enjoyed reading the *Left Behind* series by Jerry Jenkins and Tim LaHaye. Also, some books by Frank Peretti, like *Piercing the Darkness.* In addition, I like Christian music. Growing up, I always liked Michael W. Smith and Carmen. I like dc Talk, Newsboys, and Accappella.

NBA ROAD

1995: Selected by the Golden State Warriors in the second round (34th pick)

July 28, 1997: Signed by the Boston Celtics as a free agent

March 11, 1999: Traded to the Cleveland Cavaliers

THE DECLERCQ FILE

Collegiate Record
College: University of Florida

Season	Team	G	FGM	FGA	Pct.	FTM	FTA	Pct.	Reb.	Ast.	Points	Avg.
91–92	Fla	33	117	231	.506	57	87	.655	203	26	291	8.8
92–93	Fla	28	118	208	.567	59	101	.584	198	15	295	10.5
93–94	Fla	37	129	237	.544	68	104	.654	292	54	327	8.8
94–95	Fla	30	138	270	.511	115	159	.723	265	42	396	13.2
Totals		**128**	**502**	**946**	**.531**	**299**	**451**	**.663**	**958**	**137**	**1309**	**10.2**

Three-point field goals: 1993–94: 1-3 (.333); 1994–95: 5-15 (.333). **Totals:** 6-18 (.333).

NBA Record (Regular Season)

Season	Team	G	FGM	FGA	Pct.	FTM	FTA	Pct.	Reb.	Ast.	Points	Avg.
95–96	GS	22	24	50	.480	11	19	.579	39	9	59	2.7
96–97	GS	71	142	273	.520	91	151	.603	298	32	357	5.3
97–98	BOS	81	169	340	.497	101	168	.601	212	59	439	5.4
1999	B/CL	47	138	276	.500	95	141	.674	356	33	371	7.9
Totals		**221**	**473**	**939**	**.504**	**298**	**479**	**.622**	**984**	**131**	**1244**	**5.6**

Three-point field goals: 1995–96: 0-1; 1997–98: 0-1; 1999: 0-0. **Totals:** 0-2 (.000).

Bryce Drew
Beyond the Shot

VITAL STATISTICS

Bryce Homer Drew
Born: September 21, 1974, in Baton Rouge, Louisiana
6 feet 2, 188 pounds
College: Varparaiso (Indiana) University
Position: Guard
Family: Single

CAREER HONORS

- All-time Mid-Continent assists and three-point field goal leader (1998)
- Mid-Continent Male Scholar-Athlete of the Year (1998)
- All-Mid-Continent First Team (1996, 1997, 1998)

NOT-SO-VITAL STUFF

- Brother-in-law, Casey Shaw, plays for the Philadelphia 76ers
- Sister, Dana, was named Mid-American Conference Player of the Year at Toledo (twice)
- Wants to coach some day

FAVORITE VERSE

"Whatever you do, work at it with all your heart, as working for the Lord, not for men" (Colossians 3:23).

Bryce Drew

I t has to start with The Shot. Any discussion of Valparaiso's all-time best basketball player has to begin with the unpredictable, improbable, deliciously long jump shot launched by Bryce Homer Drew on March 13, 1998.

In the annals of basketball, circa 1998, there were two great shots that will forever reverberate throughout hoops history: one by a college star, the other by an NBA legend.

One, as every basketball fan with a sense of drama remembers, was Michael Jordan's picture-perfect jumper, Michael's very last game-winning shot of his career before almost 20,000 spectators. Jordan's classic door-slamming shot gave the Chicago Bulls an 87–86 victory over the Utah Jazz and put a double exclamation point on his legendary NBA stay.

Jordan's shot was typically Michaelesque, for he took the ball, faked out half the Jazz players, and created another of his textbook-style jumpers—this time even leaving his cocked wrist on display as if to say, "Fellows, if you're going to shoot the J, shoot it the MJ way."

It would be the last time fans would have a chance to marvel at Jordan's excellence.

On the other hand, there was The Shot, Bryce Drew style. Like Jordan's, it was captured on film and tape for magazine and TV highlight distribution. Like Jordan's, it won a key game, the opening round of the NCAA tournament, by one point (70–69 over the University of Mississippi). Like Jordan's, the shot was shown over and over until every detail was etched into the memory of every fan.

Both players showed great form as they squared up, leaped high, and fired the ball toward immortality. Both shots brought fans to their feet in anticipation, and the resulting brush of leather through twine launched raucous celebrations.

But there were some differences between the shots.

For Bryce Drew, the buzzer-beating shot was for him an introduction to a nation, not a farewell. Just as Jordan's shot ushered him off the stage, Drew's shot thrust him into the bright lights of national recognition.

And for Bryce Drew, the shot was not just a testament to his own personal skills, which have proven to be considerable, but was also an indication and a reminder that the Valparaiso Crusaders were directed by a pretty good coach.

While Jordan's shot was of his own making, Bryce's launch was engineered by Valparaiso's coach and Bryce's dad, Homer.

It was the end result of a play that Homer had borrowed from the Indiana Pacer playbook and had forced his players to work on over and over and over ad nauseam. The play, called "Pacer," got so tedious to Bryce after he had practiced it so often that he reportedly told his dad, "Why are we working on this? We never use it."

When Old Miss player Ansu Sesay missed a couple of free throws with 4.1 seconds to go and the Rebels clinging to a 69–67 lead, Valparaiso had the final possession. They had the length of the floor to go and just 2.5 seconds to do it.

Senior guard Jamie Sykes stood out of bounds with the ball, heaved it to Bill Jenkins, who deftly redirected the missile to a streaking Bryce. Drew grabbed it, squared, jumped, and flicked a three-pointer that made him the talk of college basketball. It was the kind of moment that even Dick Vitale couldn't have said too many superlatives about.

Somebody has to sing Bryce Drew's praise, because he certainly won't. Drew is not given to bragging. He seems instead to be a young man who is playing basketball because he loves the game, and all the things that happen to him because he is very good at it are things other people are more excited about than he is.

Of The Shot, which could send many an athlete into effusive self-tribute, Drew simply says, "It was nice that we finally got to use that play and that it worked. At the beginning, my team and I didn't look at it as anything that important. We were just happy that we had won the game."

Maybe Drew needs to see the lists of 1998 sports highlights that list The Shot (along with Michael's The Shot) in the Top 10 remarkable sports events of the year. Or maybe he has seen them and still isn't impressed. "People still come up and say, 'Yeah, you're the one that won the game with that last-second shot.' It's nice that people still remember it."

"Nice." It's a good word for Bryce to use, because that's the kind of children Homer and Janet Drew raised. Homer— who learned the ropes of coaching as Dale Brown's assistant at Louisiana State (which explains why Bryce was born in Baton Rouge) and who coached at Bethel College and Indiana-Purdue (South Bend) before taking the Valparaiso job in 1988—and Janet have three children, Dana, Scott, and Bryce.

Dana was the first of the Drew children to make a mark in sports, starring for the University of Toledo in the early nineties. She followed up her All-American status as a high school senior at Valparaiso High School with Academic All-American recognition as a guard for the Rockets.

Dana, her brothers Scott and Bryce, and their dad were backyard basketball junkies, playing two-on-two and practicing their skills. Sometimes Mom joined in or rebounded for them. All three children developed a love of basketball, which has been demonstrated in various ways.

After her career at Toledo, Dana hung around campus to work on her master's in political science. While there, she met Casey Shaw, a 6-foot-11 center with a soft outside touch (he hit 53 for 168 three-pointers during his college career). They subsequently married, and Casey was drafted by the Philadelphia 76ers in the 1998 draft.

Scott, who excelled at both tennis and basketball, was hired by his dad as his assistant coach at Valparaiso.

Bryce loved basketball at Valparaiso High, but his career nearly came to a screeching halt due to a rapid heartbeat during games. Eventually doctors settled on a form of surgery that repaired the rapid heartbeat. Otherwise, Bryce admits, "There was a chance I might not have been able to play basketball or compete athletically anymore."

That incident in Bryce's life left a lasting impression on him spiritually. He had trusted Jesus Christ as his Savior as a little child as the result of his parents' teaching. But it wasn't until the heart problem arose that he began to grow more serious about his faith. "My faith grew stronger at that point. It helped me focus my attention on God. I realized that sports could be taken away from me, and I had to turn my attention to something more permanent."

At Valparaiso High School, Bryce was a star in both basketball and tennis, although his personality didn't allow him to saunter around school like some big man on campus. His tennis game brought him considerable attention as a junior, when he made his way to the final eight singles tennis players in the state sing. As a senior, though, the accolades and honors centered on basketball.

As a player, he received the highest honor bestowed upon a high school player in the Hoosier state when he was named Mr. Basketball. As a team, Valparaiso was the number 1 ranked team in the state, and this was before Indiana switched to a system of multiclass ratings a few years ago. Bryce and Co. made it to the state finals before losing to South Bend Clay 93–88.

The college recruiting wars were a bit different around the Drew household. As a top-rated recruit, Bryce had the usual following of coaches who wanted to woo him to their school. But unlike most other high school seniors, Bryce had the factor of a father who coached at a Division I school and with whom he had a great relationship.

The irony of the situation was not lost on Homer—who was at the same time one of Bryce's recruiters and his most ardent supporter as his dad. "It was out of the norm just because he's my son," Homer says. The Drews welcomed into their home men such as John MacLeod of Notre Dame and Mike Montgomery of Stanford. "We got to meet a lot of good coaches," says the man who is noted as one himself.

Bryce agrees. "It was neat. I learned a lot through the coaches' visits. It helped me mature. And, I enjoyed my campus visits. I visited LaSalle, Syracuse, Stanford, and Notre Dame."

His parents, Bryce says, didn't try to force his decision. "My mom and dad said they were neutral. They wanted me to go somewhere that was best for me to develop as a person and as a player."

But when it came down to the time to make a decision, the influence of his parents was the deciding factor. When the Stanfords and the Syracuses of the world come calling, they can offer such things as regular NCAA tournament action and big-time TV exposure. And a player of Bryce's ability could have received greater publicity by going to a school that had already established itself as a basketball powerhouse.

At Valparaiso, he would be playing at a school with no basketball tradition. In fact, until a year before Bryce began at Valpo, the team had not had a winning mark for several years. His dad had taken over a Crusader program that was in disarray. He would suffer season records 10–19, 4–24, 5–22, 5–22, and 12–16 before he began a string of 20-victory seasons in 1993–94. So, Bryce had to have a lot of confidence that his dad was indeed building a program that would allow him to be a winner and even give him the slightest hope of attracting the attention someday of the NBA.

As Bryce remembers it, though, none of those things could sway his decision, which he says was based on "my family, my brother, and my dad."

It turned out to be the right decision. Bryce was the key factor in a Crusader run that was nothing short of remarkable. During the four years he attended Valparaiso, the team compiled an 88–36 record. What's more, the Crusaders did something no one had ever done: They won their regular season conference title and their conference tournament four years in a row. Bryce Drew's contribution to that success was considerable.

- Named a first team All-Mid-Continent player during his sophomore, junior, and senior years
- Selected the Mid-Continent Tournament MVP three years (1995, 1997, 1998)
- Ranked ninth in the nation in free-throw shooting with a 87.9 percentage during his junior year
- Selected as a third team All-American during his senior year
- Made 364 three-point field goals at college, placing him sixth all-time in NCAA records

For three straight years, Valparaiso made it to the NCAA tournament behind Bryce Drew. The first year was a nightmare for the new kids on the block. Playing fifth-ranked Arizona, the Crusaders were destroyed, 90–51. But Bryce saw a clear benefit. "That kind of turned me and the whole team around. That gave us extra motivation."

The next season, the Crusaders came back for more. This time, their draw was a bit kinder: Boston College, the 20th-ranked team. The Eagles were 21–8 heading into the tournament against the 24–6 Crusaders. They were a number 5 seed up against Valparaiso's 12th seed. Bryce was right on form that day, scoring 27 points, including eight three-pointers. But Boston College went away with the victory, 73–66.

Which brings us to the 1998 tournament and Bryce's heroics against Ole Miss. After that big game, which surprised everyone, the Crusaders were not through. Their next giant to take on was Florida State. A win against the Seminoles would put the team into the Sweet Sixteen, quite an accomplishment for a school with just 3,000 students.

Hope reigned in northwest Indiana when Valpo rallied from a big deficit in that game to force the Seminoles into overtime. In the extra stanza, the Crusaders cruised, eventually beating Florida State 83–77.

Suddenly people around the country were wondering. Who is this team, and could they possibly sneak into the Elite Eight . . . or maybe even the Final Four?

At the Midwest regional, Valparaiso played Rhode Island close but could not catch them at the end, losing finally 74–67. It was the end of an incredible run for Valparaiso and an unbelievable career for Bryce Drew.

Could all that attention and adulation change Bryce Drew? The national media, including ESPN and Fox TV, appeared on campus as the Crusaders moved deeper into the tournament. The spotlight shone on Drew, "but it really wasn't that big of an adjustment," the player reports, "because I just went on living the way I had always been living." Which means the quiet life of a future NBA first-round draft pick who is a local legend and who made the biggest shot in school history.

Draft day was pretty much like most of the things Bryce Drew is involved in. A family thing. "I was with my mom, my dad, and my brother," he says, surprising no one.

One member of the family, though, was not there. Dana and her husband, Casey, decided they would spend draft day elsewhere. He too was slated to be picked in the draft, so Bryce and his brother-in-law felt it best not to be going through the tension together.

When the announcement was made on TV that the Houston Rockets had picked Bryce, he saw it at the same time as the rest of North America. "I found out on TV just like everyone else," he says. And he was happy with the team he was going to be signing to play for.

"I was definitely happy with Houston. I liked it a lot when I went down to work out. I think I fit into their system well. Also, I was happy because they drafted Michael Dickerson [an Arizona star], and I knew he was a Christian. And Brent Price is there, another Christian. I was happy to know they were also going to be there."

But before Drew had the opportunity to sign that first contract and get acquainted with his new teammates, he had to sit out the first work stoppage in NBA history. "It was a stressful few months there," he says of the lockout. "About all I was doing was living in the gym and working out. I wanted to make sure I was in shape. I wanted to give it my best shot. There are so many good players out there, and not many get drafted. I feel really blessed to be drafted."

Drew's first year in the NBA was a mixture of high expectations, average success, and lots of learning. In a season that must have seemed like a ride on an out-of-control freight train because of its 50-games-in-90-days pace, Drew had enough highlights to whet his appetite for what lies ahead.

In the Rockets' first three games in his rookie year, Bryce averaged 20 minutes and 6 points—hitting 8 points against Golden State in only his second NBA contest. Although he began the year as backup to Matt Maloney at point, things changed. First Maloney was hurt, then Cuttino Mobley won the favor of the coaching staff. Playing time was sometimes rare for Drew on a team with four point guards (Drew, Maloney, Mobley, and Brent Price).

Drew's first year didn't give him All-Star stats, but he showed enough savvy and game smarts to impress the not-easy-to-impress Charles Barkley. Of Bryce, Sir Charles said, "He'll do fine. He's a good kid who really knows the game."

Bryce Drew has quietly developed a reputation as a winner. He would never boast of his success, and he doesn't have it in him to strut and swagger about the skills God has given him. He's quiet and given to short answers when being interviewed, but it's not rudeness or brusqueness. It's the simple fact that Bryce Drew, the man who hit the shot that rivaled Michael Jordan for Big Moment in Hoops in 1998, is just the kind of man you'd expect Homer and Janet Drew's son to be: talented, humble, and polite—with a quiet confidence that never becomes cockiness.

Someday, perhaps, he'll hit other baskets that will rival The Shot. That remains to be seen. But if he doesn't, two things are clear. One, he'll be content with the way life is treating him. And two, he'll still be eager to credit God with the success and happiness that have come his way.

Q & A WITH BRYCE DREW

Q: *What is the best spiritual advice you've received?*
Bryce: Make sure at every second of your life you know God is in control. Because if anything would happen, you know you are going to heaven. I guess some people are unsure, and they wait until they are older to give their life to Christ, but don't wait; do it right away. You want to make sure you get to heaven.

Q: *Your favorite verse is Colossians 3:23: "Whatever you do, work at it with all your heart, as working for the Lord, not for men." Why?*
Bryce: During the time when I wanted to get into the NBA, I think I was trying to impress people instead of playing for God. That verse helped me to put my focus on Him, and that He's the audience I'm playing for.

Q: *What do you think is the best way to stay strong spiritually?*
Bryce: One thing that helps is hanging around other believers. I think they can encourage you and also show you the right way. So find some good Christian friends, and do things with them.

Q: *Who were your sports heroes when you were younger?*
Bryce: I really liked Dave Kingman, because he played for the Cubs, and I'm a baseball fan. I guess when I was in high school, I liked Tony Bennett, a Christian NBA player who played for the Charlotte Hornets. His dad coached at University of Wisconsin at Green Bay, and he played for his dad, so we had that in common. We've talked a lot, and he has really helped me out a lot.

Q: *What effect does your faith have on you as a basketball player?*
Bryce: I think that the first thing it does is keep things in perspective. It helps me to realize that it is just a game and to know that there is more to life than just going out and playing the minutes on the floor. The other thing is it makes me play harder, because I know that God has blessed me to have an opportunity to play. I don't take it for granted being out there. I

think that makes me more intense and want to play harder than other people would.

Q: *What kind of ministries do you like to be involved in?*
Bryce: I would say the biggest thing would be to be a good example. Being a pro athlete, anything you do, people are going to see. I just want to make sure I set a good example for people.

I've thought about having a camp in the future. Also, I've been helping out a pastor who has an after-school program. It's run by a church. I help with that. . . .

I also enjoy speaking to youth groups, especially the high school age because that's a big time in people's lives when they make a decision, either to start to go astray or start to build up stronger in the faith.

NBA ROAD

1998: Selected by the Houston Rockets in the first round of the draft

THE DREW FILE

Collegiate Record
College: Valparaiso University

Season	Team	G	FGM	FGA	Pct.	FTM	FTA	Pct.	Reb.	Ast.	Points	Avg.
94–95	Valpo	27	117	267	.438	49	65	.754	64	162	361	13.4
95–96	Valpo	32	178	401	.444	103	119	.866	92	164	551	17.2
96–97	Valpo	31	193	419	.461	131	149	.879	94	145	617	19.9
97–98	Valpo	31	208	462	.450	103	130	.792	130	155	613	19.8
Totals		**121**	**696**	**1549**	**.449**	**386**	**463**	**.834**	**380**	**626**	**2142**	**17.7**

Three-point field goals: 1994–95: 78-170 (.459); 1995–96: 92-231 (.398); 1996–97: 100-217 (.457); 1997–98: 94-217 (.433). **Totals:** 364-837 (.435).

NBA Record (Regular Season)

Season	Team	G	FGM	FGA	Pct.	FTM	FTA	Pct.	Reb.	Ast.	Points	Avg.
1999	HOU	34	47	129	.364	8	9	1.000	31	52	118	3.5

Three-point field goals: 1999: 16-49 (.327).

But then trouble struck, first for LaPhonso, and then for the Nuggets. On September 11, Ellis suffered a stress fracture to the patella in his right knee. After two months of rest didn't heal the knee, he had surgery on November 22, virtually wiping out the 1994–95 season. He would appear in just six games for the Nuggets that season. The Nuggets finished 41–41 that season, but that's as close as they would get to a good season during the rest of the twentieth century.

First, they lost Robert Pack in a trade to Washington; Abdul-Rauf followed via the trade route to Sacramento. Then Mutombo went to Atlanta as a free agent. In the meantime, over the next few years, talented and respected young players such as Tommy Hammonds, Jalen Rose, and Antonio McDyess, came and went.

And Ellis, upon whom so much of Denver's success depended, suffered another injury in 1997, this time a ruptured Achilles tendon.

From 1995–96 through 1997–1998, the team began a free fall, winning 35, 21, and finally an embarrassing 11 games, respectively. To LaPhonso, the destruction of his once hopeful team meant the bottom had dropped out of his promising basketball career.

"I went down with the injury, and we had an even-par season the following year. Then we ended up trading away or allowing all of our assets that made our team good to leave. It was just a waste to see."

In one sense, it doesn't seem right to begin a recounting of LaPhonso Ellis's life by talking about something so negative as his career low point and the Nuggets' troubles. Indeed, LaPhonso is anything but negative.

The face of the big, strong forward smiles from the media guide. In the Ellis family portrait, a bright-eyed daddy holds his laughing son while his smiling wife holds their clearly happy daughter. Listen to him talk, and you hear a frequent laugh, one that comes not from nervousness or from foolish humor but from a heart that is genuinely content.

One writer, trying to explain the calm with which LaPhonso Ellis faced the storm of being a leader on a team that was

11–71, called the big man from East St. Louis, Illinois, a "true professional in the face of adversity."

Yes, it is appropriate to bring up the less-than-triumphant situation LaPhonso faced in the late nineties in Denver, because he is the kind of person who can teach anyone who will listen how to face life's bad times.

At the base of Ellis's ability to smile—even laugh—in the face of adversity is his faith. "We have to understand that this is a life that we are just passing through," he begins, as he explains his philosophy. "We have to ask the Lord for strength and courage to overcome a lot of obstacles. That's why a relationship with our Lord Jesus is so important. I know that is the number one thing that got me through all of those problems.

"We have to remember who we are living for. In basketball, we have to remember who we are playing for. I've been asked, 'Did you ever get frustrated and want to give it up?' I never had that because I didn't feel God was moving me to do anything else at that time. I just felt strongly He was calling me to do what I had to do."

In order to get back to playing form, Ellis had to endure a rigorous and often painful rehabilitation period for each injury. Hour upon hour was spent away from the team, lifting weights or running—just pushing himself to the limit. All the while, his team was losing and he couldn't do anything about it.

"It was so frustrating," he recalls. "Talk about tedious and monotonous! It was awful! But to be able to look up and know that one day God would possibly reward me for the hard work I was putting in at the time—that kept me going. And on a day-to-day basis I asked Him for strength and focus to make it through. I gave Him an honest effort every day."

For LaPhonso, the physical reward for his hard work came on the court during the 1996–97 season. Although the team was in the middle of one of its bad seasons, Ellis showed everyone that he could come back. In 55 games that season, he averaged 22 points a game. Many had predicted LaPhonso would never play again. Yet had he played a few more games, he would have qualified as one of the Top 10 scorers in the league. "So far, that has been the pinnacle of my career," says the big forward of his comeback. "To see the result of all that hard work was just phenomenal."

Hard work and tough circumstances have been the trademark of LaPhonso's life. The son of a single mom who raised LaPhonso and his brother LeRoy by herself with the help of tough love, dedication, a strong work ethic, and the assistance of government programs, Ellis can never shake the lessons such a life taught him.

One Thanksgiving, LaPhonso and his wife, Jennifer, were working at a homeless shelter in Denver, packing Thanksgiving dinners for people who might otherwise go without a big meal on the big day. A high school group from a church came to visit the shelter, and the Nuggets forward turned into a tour guide, showing them around the warehouse.

"I became a little emotional when I saw the USDA [United States Department of Agriculture] government assistance boxes back there. It reminded me of my childhood and how thankful I am. If it wasn't for the help of the government, I don't think I would have survived.

"We were really, really poor. My mom worked a job or two at a time to put food on the table for us."

As a youngster growing up that way, LaPhonso had absolutely no idea, no dream, no inkling that basketball might be his ticket out of poverty. He didn't play for that reason. He just liked it.

By the time he had reached East St. Louis Lincoln High School, though, "people began to say that I might be something special. I tend to be humble about my outlook on myself, and I never thought I'd turn out to be very much. I was a good student, and I felt that because I was a good student, I would be able to get a decent job and earn a good living as I got older. But I never thought I would have an opportunity to play college basketball—and certainly not go on to play professional basketball."

No matter what LaPhonso thought, by the time he was a junior in high school, enough major college coaches had contacted him that he finally realized he had a shot at playing in college.

Either way, Ellis would have probably done OK for himself, thanks to Mom. "I was a good kid, but a lot of that was because my mother kept me away from temptation. I had to be in the house before the lights were on, and she always put academics first. If I didn't do well, she would pull me from the team."

After graduating from Lincoln High, and before he took off for South Bend to play basketball for Digger Phelps at Notre Dame, LaPhonso did some business with God. That summer, he trusted Jesus Christ as Savior and was baptized. "I wanted to give my life to the Lord. It was very personal. The Holy Spirit moved me to accept the Lord that summer," he says.

It would be a while, though, before LaPhonso would understand completely what it means to live for Jesus each day. In fact, it wasn't until he got to the professional level that true spiritual growth began to take place. "I was probably more of a typical college student," he says, looking back on his years with the Fighting Irish. "I was a shelf Christian going through college. I would only get into it when I found myself in a tight spot."

While at Notre Dame, Ellis helped the Irish out of several tight spots with his scoring and rebounding. When Notre Dame earned a spot in the NCAA tournament, and the adrenaline was flowing, "I grabbed 17 or 18 rebounds and we beat Vanderbilt," LaPhonso recalls. "I just don't remember jumping higher than I jumped that night." He calls that performance his college highlight.

But he also likes to think about a series of games three years later, during his final season at Notre Dame. The Fighting Irish, then under the tutelage of John MacLeod, was already 1–5 and beginning a long road trip that included University of Southern California (USC), LaSalle (both Top 20 teams), and North Carolina (UNC). A 1–8 start didn't look like an impossibility.

But then "everything started to change," LaPhonso says. In the two biggest games of the road trip, against USC and UNC, Ellis showed everyone watching that he was a bona fide star. Against USC, he scored 27 points and grabbed 18 rebounds. A few days later, the Fighting Irish played the Tar Heels at Madison Square Garden on national TV. Ellis led Notre Dame to victory with 31 points and 12 rebounds. The folks at NBC named him their Player of the Game.

That senior season, the Fighting Irish were an enigma. LaPhonso says, "Against the teams we were supposed to beat, we lost. The teams we were supposed to lose to, we beat." Apparently, they didn't play enough of those teams, because Notre Dame was not picked to play in the NCAA tournament field. However, the NIT invited them. The Irish made it to the NIT Finals, which meant they played again at Madison Square Garden. Against Virginia, Notre Dame lost, ending Ellis's college career.

LaPhonso came away from Notre Dame with more than a degree in accounting. He also came away with his future bride. Jennifer was a student at St. Mary's College, which is situated across the street from Notre Dame in South Bend. She, like LaPhonso, was from a poor family, and although they wanted to get married while he was still in college, they couldn't afford to. As a scholarship player, he had some stipulations in his deal with the college—guidelines that said he would lose some of his scholarship privileges if he were to marry.

So, Jennifer and LaPhonso delayed their wedding until August 1992, well after LaPhonso knew he would be employed soon by the Denver Nuggets.

"I had no idea the Nuggets were going to pick me," he says as he recalls the NBA draft day. He was present for the selection, since he was slated as a probable first-round pick. "Right as we were getting ready for the fifth pick, my agent came over and told me Denver was picking me fifth. Being a 'bird-in-the-hand' kind of guy, I said, 'Okay, sure.' Then they said my name. It was an overwhelming feeling."

For a kid whose mom had given up so much to help him succeed and who had waited two years to marry his college sweetheart, it was a special time. "I felt a strong responsibility to take care of my mom and Jennifer. There were a number of issues that were burdens on my shoulders. Those burdens were relieved the day I was drafted."

Ellis did not disappoint the people who signed him to a

contract that would alleviate his money problems and allow him to care for the important people in his life. He burst on the NBA scene in 1992–93 by earning a starting spot on the Nuggets squad. Several times during the year he led the team in scoring. The first time was a clear indication that the Nuggets had a star in Ellis. He scored 27 points against the L.A. Clippers on November 28, 1992. He became the first Nugget rookie ever to start all 82 games.

The numbers continued to improve in the 1993–94 season. In a game against Boston, he scored a career-high 29 points. Against Houston, he grabbed 19 rebounds. His scoring average rose to 15.4 points per game. Clearly, the road ahead looked like a Montana interstate on a summer day. Nothing could stand between him and stardom.

Nothing but a bum knee. The knee he injured in September 1994. The injury that would curtail his play for the next two seasons. And the knee that helped him spiritually. Ellis explains: "I didn't take the Word of God seriously until all the knee problems happened. I felt that God was saying to me, 'You can't serve Me and the world. You have to do one or the other.'"

Fortunately LaPhonso had someone in Denver to guide him through the struggles of career-threatening injuries, Bo Mitchell, the longtime chaplain for the Nuggets. Mitchell stayed beside Ellis through the ordeal, continually encouraging him to trust Christ with His difficulty. "Bo held my hand through the fire," LaPhonso explains. "He passed me on to Jesus, and I've been running one step behind Him every since."

As Ellis seeks to grow stronger in his faith, he learns valuable lessons about God and His work in a life. "I am learning to understand year by year how God uses adversity to bring you closer to Him. I'm learning that God uses adversity to say, 'Here I am; I want you closer.' For whatever reason, I have a responsibility to help others face adversity. I take that very seriously."

Ellis also takes his spiritual growth seriously. He and Jennifer have found valuable ways to keep their relationship with Jesus Christ strong. For Jennifer, much of her growth comes in the small-group environment of Bible Study Fellowship.

At one time, she was studying the Old Testament in BSF while her husband was studying the New Testament on his own. "She was able to give me a lot of information with respect to the Old Testament, and that was great."

For his individual growth progress, LaPhonso sets this pattern: "I typically read and study one chapter a night in an *NIV Life Application Study Bible*. I read the chapter and meditate on it. Then I read the verse-by-verse description to clarify any issues I may have had. If I miss one night, I feel off balance the next day."

In addition, LaPhonso has found one radio preacher, Charles Stanley, to be especially helpful, so he listens to him whenever possible.

The opportunity to fellowship with other Christians has also grown more important to Ellis as he has grown spiritually. During the lockout before the 1999 season, he found three Christians with whom he could work out to stay in shape. One was a former NBA player, another was fresh out of college, and the other had suffered an injury that would keep him out of the league.

"I prayed that the Lord would bring some Christian individuals into my life, and He brought these three guys to be my workout partners."

As a member of the Denver Nuggets, LaPhonso Ellis was forced to sink with the team to the depths of trouble. Yet his spirit never sank with the team's demise. Ironically, through his personal, physical struggles as well as the team's poverty of success, he was growing spiritually. He came through the fiery furnace of difficulties with an increased faith, a better appetite for God's Word, and a more serious outlook on his relationship with Christ.

Sure, it doesn't seem fair that a nice guy like LaPhonso Ellis should have been stuck in a not-so-nice situation as he found himself, but obviously God knew he needed the challenge.

Now, he's the kind of NBA player to whom people can look with admiration, whether he is winning or losing. He's the kind of man whose faith affects his game so much that he can say, "I'm consciously thinking about my testimony in a game. When there's an opponent who may be shorter or a little less talented, I'm always conscious of treating that person with the utmost respect. Even when I'm playing against a person who is better than I am, I'm always making sure I'm playing the game fairly."

For a man who's been through what LaPhonso Ellis has been through, it's nice to know that he can say, "We aren't responsible for what happens to us, but we are called to be incredibly responsible for our response to whatever the situation is. I try to take that seriously."

That kind of attitude helped Jennifer and La Phonso in early 1999 when they realized Denver would not be re-signing him. The couple spent much time praying for God's guidance. Eventually they felt led to a new home, as LaPhonso signed with the Atlanta Hawks.

What more can you ask from a Christian professional athlete than to trust God and to follow His guidance?

Q & A WITH LAPHONSO ELLIS

Q: *What kind of music do you like?*
LaPhonso: I started the weeding-out process about a year ago. Having kids changes your music tastes in a hurry. Obviously some of the music you don't want their ears to hear. I feel strongly that I need to be a good steward with the children that the Lord has blessed me with. I have to make sure that what I'm teaching them is consistent with the way I'm living my life, so I'm taking a lot of music out of my collection and trying to purify it. We actually bought my daughter some Christian artists. I got her some Out of Eden and Jaci Velasquez. We're making the conversion.

Q: *Does it come naturally for you to share your faith with others?*
LaPhonso: About three months ago, I was struggling with sharing my faith in terms of knowing what to say, and I came across a verse of Scripture that says to share what the Lord has done for you. He's done so many wonderful things for me that it's easy to share my faith now.

Q: *After the lockout of 1998–99, what do the players have to do to win the fans back?*

LaPhonso: I feel that everyone follows a winner, and I feel that if we get back to doing the things that turned the league from a drug-infested, noninteresting league to where we have been over the past ten or fifteen years, I think the fans will come back. Everyone loves a good product. I think the NBA has to start being more responsible and not allowing the coverage to go toward the guys who are struggling with different adversities. They need to put forward the David Robinsons and A. C. Greens of our world, those guys who are full of integrity in front of the international audience. People want to identify with goodness, and if you get those quality people . . . doing your interviews and over the television, then I think that will serve the image of the NBA quite well.

Q: *What is one thing you wish NBA fans knew about NBA players?*

LaPhonso: That pro athletes are real people who have real struggles in life. Even though [the players] exist under an umbrella called NBA basketball with the glitz and glamour and dollars associated with it, a lot of these people have real world problems, and they have a lot of people they are responsible for. The media, all they really write is what is so wrong with our world, and there is so much that is so right about our league.

NBA ROAD

1992: Selected by the Denver Nuggets in the first round of the draft

1999: Signed by the Atlanta Hawks as a free agent on January 30, 1999

THE ELLIS FILE

Collegiate Record

College: University of Notre Dame

Season	Team	G	FGM	FGA	Pct.	FTM	FTA	Pct.	Reb.	Ast.	Points	Avg.
88–89	ND	27	156	277	.563	52	76	.684	254	31	365	13.5
89–90	ND	22	114	223	.511	79	117	.675	278	33	309	14.0
90–91	ND	15	90	157	.573	58	81	.716	158	26	246	16.4
91–92	ND	33	227	360	.631	127	194	.655	385	51	585	17.7
Totals		**97**	**587**	**1017**	**.577**	**316**	**468**	**.675**	**1075**	**141**	**1505**	**15.5**

Three-point field goals: 1988–89: 1-1; 1989–90: 2-6 (.333); 1990–91: 8-17 (.471); 1991—92: 4-9 (.444). **Totals:** 15-33 (.455).

NBA Record (Regular Season)

Season	Team	G	FGM	FGA	Pct.	FTM	FTA	Pct.	Reb.	Ast.	Points	Avg.
92–93	DEN	82	483	958	.504	237	327	.748	744	151	1205	14.7
93–94	DEN	79	483	963	.502	242	359	.674	682	167	1215	15.4
94–95	DEN	6	9	25	.360	6	6	1.000	17	4	24	4.0
95–96	DEN	45	189	432	.438	89	148	.601	322	74	471	10.5
96–97	DEN	44	445	1014	.439	218	282	.773	386	131	1203	21.9
97–98	DEN	76	410	1007	.407	206	256	.805	544	213	1083	14.3
1999	ATL	20	80	190	.421	43	61	.705	110	18	204	10.2
Totals		**363**	**2099**	**4589**	**.457**	**1041**	**1429**	**.728**	**1932**	**758**	**5405**	**14.9**

Three-point field goals: 1992–93: 2-13 (.154); 1993–94: 7-23 (.304); 1995–96: 4-22 (.182); 1996–97: 95-259 (.367); 1997–98: 57-201 (.284); 1999: 1-5 (.200). **Totals:** 166-523 (.317).

Todd Fuller
Stats and Stuff

VITAL STATISTICS

Todd Douglas Fuller
Born: July 25, 1974, in Fayetteville, North Carolina
6 feet 11, 255 pounds
College: North Carolina State
Position: Center
Family: Single

CAREER HONORS

- In his first game with the Jazz, scored 10 points and grabbed 3 rebounds (1999)
- Named Payne Webber Scholar-Athlete of the Year (1996)
- Voted to Atlantic Coast Conference First Team (1996)
- Selected Academic All-American (1995)

NOT-SO-VITAL STUFF

- Enjoys tennis, golf, and computer games
- As a kid, liked Kevin McHale and Larry Bird
- In his senior year at North Carolina State he had a 3.97 GPA

FAVORITE VERSES

"'For I know the plans I have for you,' declares the Lord, 'plans to prosper you and not to harm you, plans to give you hope and a future'" (Jeremiah 29:11).

"Do not be anxious about anything, but in everything, by prayer and petition, with thanksgiving, present your requests to God. And the peace of God, which transcends all understanding, will guard your hearts and your minds in Christ Jesus" (Philippians 4:6–7).

Todd Fuller

Basketball players love statistics. They love to know how many points they scored, what their average is, what the team's winning percentage is, how many rebounds they are getting a game. Players who are getting paid to play basketball are even more acutely aware of statistics, because they know that their numbers can add up to millions of dollars—another popular statistic—for them.

Todd Fuller is no exception in the statistics department. He knows the numbers about himself, and he understands their importance. But when it comes to statistics, he is in a class by himself among NBA players. That's because he thinks it might be his goal after his basketball playing days to go to graduate school and spend countless hours listening to professors talk about, reading books about, and studying statistics.

There's something about this that we need to get clear right away, though. This does not mean he will sit in a grad school and figure out the Boston Celtics' shooting percentage. No, we're talking *real* statistics. As in this explanation from *Grolier's Encyclopedia:*

> Statistics is the science of collecting and analyzing data. Whether some natural phenomenon is being observed or a scientific experiment is being carried out, the analysis will

be statistical if it is impossible to predict the data exactly with certainty. On a trivial level, consider the tossing of a coin. If it is double-headed, then the experiment is deterministic, or nonrandom, because it can be predicted confidently that the coin will land "heads" up. If it is a regular coin, however, the experiment is a random, or chance-influenced, phenomenon; the coin may land "heads" or "tails." Statistics can be more precisely defined as the collection and analysis of data from random experiments or phenomena.

Say what?

That's the kind of stuff Todd Fuller hopes to get his master's degree in someday.

For now, though, the former Rhodes Scholar nominee who graduated from North Carolina State with a bachelor of science in applied mathematics, with a grade point average just a couple of Bs short of 4.00, is too busy living out his lifelong dream to worry about means and modes, variance and covariance, and matters relating to standards of deviation.

Being a statistician is what someone with Fuller's aptitude might end up doing because he has to make a living at something he's good at.

Being a pro basketball player is what a Carolina kid with big dreams does because it's in his blood.

"I had dreamed about the NBA since I was eight," Todd says, and you get the feeling he could tell you the date he first had that dream if you were to ask him for it. "I remember in elementary school we had to do a project in which we had to write up an obituary on ourselves. I put in there that I had become an NBA player. It's funny, looking back on that dream after achieving it. It was just a dream, all the way until my junior year of college—when I realized my dream was close to becoming a reality."

Doug and Sheryl Fuller of Matthews, North Carolina, had two children, Todd and his older sister, Lynn, who is now a music teacher. Todd and Lynn's parents were athletes in their own right. Both of them played high school ball, and Doug played small college hoops. So from an early age, they encouraged their son in a variety of sports activities. It's a good thing they were behind his sporting efforts, because he spent much of his time involved in sports as a youngster.

Todd loved swimming and spent nine years on different swim teams. He played guard in football for a couple of years. He was a goalie in soccer and played third base and pitched in baseball. He also played tennis. As Todd puts it, "I was very active."

Yet he wasn't a one-dimensional kid who gave up everything else to pursue sports. He participated in music in school, and still he excelled in the classroom.

"I loved computers. I started getting an interest in them in the fifth grade. We had an Apple II computer in the classroom, and I fell in love with it. That's how that all started."

Eventually, he even built a computer. Well, he claims he didn't really build it. "I never built my own computer from scratch," he explains before he clarifies. "Well, I put the components together. It's not hard to do." For a future scholar-athlete of the year, perhaps.

"You can buy a motherboard and a case. If you follow directions and are patient, almost anybody can do it. Put the cards in there, along with the RAM and memory chips. Things like that."

Oh.

Perhaps "kind of" building a computer from parts is not that surprising anymore—what with an entire generation growing up not knowing that there was ever a time when the words "ram" and "mouse" meant nothing but some kind of animal. So if assembling a computer doesn't sound especially remarkable, how about this: Todd built a hovercraft when he was a high school senior.

By then, Todd was no longer the play-everything sports aficionado he had been, for he had turned his athletic concentration over to basketball. And he had taken his considerable size and rapidly improving skills to Charlotte Christian High School. There, he came under the direction of one of the best defensive basketball players ever: Bobby Jones.

Jones, who had played in the old American Basketball Association before moving to the NBA, was the proud owner of an NBA championship ring—earned as a member of the 1983 Philadelphia 76ers. He had settled with his wife, Tess, and their children in Charlotte, where Bobby was creating a basketball dynasty of sorts at Charlotte Christian.

During Todd's junior year at Independence High School, he visited Charlotte Christian. Unable to decide whether to transfer, Todd didn't finally choose to spend his senior year playing for Bobby Jones until one week before school started.

When he did begin at Charlotte Christian, he stood in awe of the former NBA first team All-Defense performer. "I was literally shaking when I met him for the first time," Fuller says.

Of course, when a 6-foot-10 kid transfers in for his senior year, everyone expects he has just one thing on his mind: basketball. But Fuller was never a single-dimensional person. He proved that by what he did in his physics class during his last few months of school—building that hovercraft.

By then, he had accomplished all he could on the basketball court. Todd had averaged 22.8 points for Coach Jones to go along with his 16 rebounds and 4 blocked shots a game. Behind Fuller, Charlotte Christian won the North Carolina independent school state championship. In one game, he scored 47 points. In another, he ripped down 24 rebounds. There wasn't anything left for him to do but sign his letter of intent and get ready to move his stuff to Raleigh and see what he could do for the North Carolina State Wolfpack.

However, there was this little thing called graduation on the horizon, and that meant classes like physics. And in physics class, everyone had to do some kind of project. The teacher suggested someone build a hovercraft.

The general response from the class was, "Yeah, right! There's no way!" But as time rolled around to pick a project to do, Fuller saw some potential in the teacher's idea. "I couldn't think of anything else to do," he says, "so I took him up on the offer."

The teacher explained to Todd what he would have to do if he wanted to build this fly-through-the-air device, even down to telling him that he would have to find an Electrolux vacuum cleaner motor.

Fuller found one, took it home, and actually built a hovercraft. It wasn't like he could ride it to Raleigh or anything, but it did what it was designed to do. "My sister and I both stood on the thing, and it held us up." Then he took it to school and demonstrated it in front of the physics class. "One of the students got on the thing and we pushed him around the classroom, riding on the hovercraft."

Clearly, it seemed, academically and athletically, Fuller was ready for college.

Yet as he reviews those next few years, he feels he could have been better off to spend another year at Charlotte Christian.

"After the 1998 NBA season, Coach Jones and I were talking about the past few years. I said that if I had to do it all over again, I would have stayed back an extra year. Coach was nodding his head, and I said, 'What are you nodding your head for?' He said, 'I told you you should have stayed back when you first came to Charlotte Christian.'"

Though Fuller was a powerful player and clearly an intelligent athlete, he was only seventeen years old on graduation day. He figures one more year of high school before heading off to college and eventually the NBA would have left him more prepared. He probably could have used another year of spiritual growth as well. Todd clearly acknowledges that he was not exactly tearing the world up spiritually through his high school days.

At age nine, Todd Fuller began to think seriously about faith in Christ. He had attended Sunday school and church for some time and remembers one Sunday school teacher "who was very good. He did a great job of relating to kids our age. Over a period of time of being under his direction, we understood what he was saying. He explained what it means to have a relationship with Jesus Christ. On my own, I remember bowing my head in my room at home in October 1983 and praying to trust Jesus. A couple of times in the class, the teacher had invited anybody in the class who had not made the decision to accept

Christ to do so. But I never did that in class. I wanted to think about it."

Despite his newfound faith, it would be a number of years before he would begin to take it seriously. "All the way through junior high, high school, and much of college, I took my faith for granted. When I went off to NC State, that's when my faith really started to grow. God put in my life people for whom having Christ in their life is so important."

One of the keys to this new growth as a believer came to Todd when he saw the number of activities a Christian could get involved with at NC State. "When I got to State, I was surprised at how much action there was for Christ on campus. It was just amazing how the Lord led me in the right direction." He credits three elements with his drawing close to Christ: those committed Christians, life experiences, and a new motivation to grow spiritually.

Thus encouraged and motivated to make the most of his faith, Todd also grew increasingly motivated by what was happening on the basketball floor. In each of his four years with the Wolfpack, he got better, even though by his own admission he didn't exactly make Dick Vitale's mouth drop open in his first couple of years.

"When I was a freshman at NC State, I had a very slow start. Things weren't [going] well for me or for my team." But things got better. "By the end of my junior year, I started to realize that a dream of mine was about to come true."

A closer look at his four years at NC State bears out what he was saying. As a freshman, he made second team on the All-Atlantic Coast Conference freshman squad. His sophomore year was better, as he averaged 11.8 points and 8 rebounds per game as a full-time starter. For his accomplishments, he was named to the All-ACC third team.

But it was in his junior year that he began to raise NBA eyebrows. He raised his scoring to 16 points a game and was voted to the All-ACC second team. In what was a highlight game his junior year, he scored 30 points against Wake Forest and Tim Duncan.

His continual improvement reflected an important lesson

Coach Jones had taught him while he was still in high school.

"He taught me the value of a consistent effort over a long period of time," Fuller says. "Coach Jones had a Bible lesson for us two or three times a week before practice. I remember one time Coach Jones was talking about the value of investing, like in a bank account. It grows over time. Like in basketball or anything else, you invest that time and effort little by little, on a consistent basis. That will grow over time."

So Fuller continued to maintain his intensity at North Carolina State. On the court that meant that his senior year would be his best. Buoyed by his dream, his growing success, and his consistent faith, he put together the kind of year he would need to get a high pick in the draft. Fuller made first-team All-ACC, he ranked third in the ACC in field-goal shooting and free-throw shooting percentage, and he led the Wolfpack in scoring all but three games.

He had the stats that would clearly answer any questions about which postgrad work he would be getting into next. Clearly, getting into the NBA would take precedence over getting an M.A. It was time to travel to New Jersey for the 1996 NBA draft.

"It was a fun week," he says. Besides holding the draft in the Meadowlands in New Jersey (where the Nets play), the NBA flew the players and their families up. The Fullers spent a couple days in New York City and saw plays on Broadway, courtesy of the NBA. Then his family and friends applauded loudly when Todd went to the Golden State Warriors as the eleventh pick of the draft.

Todd's first years in the NBA were similar to his first years in college. Lower numbers and lots of learning going on. Lots of opportunities to test Coach Jones's theories about investing.

"We live in such an instant society," Fuller says. "Too many people want to have success right away without really earning it or doing the little things every day to make success a reality. Coach Jones taught me that if I was patient and worked hard, good things would happen."

In his first two years in the league, Fuller averaged 4 points a game in the 132 contests he played in, yet he was not willing to give up and say that's all he could do.

"The first two years were rocky for me," he explains. "The hardest adjustment coming in was defensively. The worst player in the NBA can score. You've got guys who can flat out eat you alive if you are not ready for them. Especially down in the paint. Guys are so big, so strong, so agile."

While learning the ropes on the court and adjusting to players who are bigger, faster, and stronger, Fuller also learned about some of the intangibles that are not understood or appreciated by those who aren't on the inside of the NBA looking out. What he learned helped him to think again about the importance of strong faith.

"When I looked at the NBA growing up," he says, "I thought it was all glamour. It's an awesome occupation, and I wouldn't trade it for the world, but when you get involved with it, there are tons of ups and downs—just like any other job. Maybe even more so, because winning is the life and blood of pro basketball.

"It's so easy to be tossed around like a wave if you allow things like playing time and wins and losses to affect you. Also, being away from home for long periods of time is not good.

"Being in the NBA and thinking about these things helped me to grow in my faith. I realized that I had to keep my faith in Christ. I can remember driving home from the arena in my first couple of years. Perhaps we didn't play well and we lost the game, or I didn't play much or at all that particular game. I would pray as I drove back home in the car. I would pray that I would keep things in perspective. It's a constant challenge not to let basketball be tied in to your self-worth."

"I think in many ways it was God's way of saying, 'Look, you need to have your faith in Me and not in your basketball ability.' The basketball ability can come and go. In fact, He can take it away from me in a moment's notice if He wanted to. I slowly began to realize that my faith had to be in Christ. Otherwise, I could wake up one day feeling like a million bucks and the next day feeling like junk because of the way basketball was going. That was not a healthy way of living."

It might have been easier for Todd Fuller to take the NCAA up on their offer to give him a postgraduate scholarship. There, he could have studied statistics instead of trying to pile them up against Shaquille O'Neal and Dikembe Mutombo. There, he wouldn't have had to worry about those long drives home after a loss. He wouldn't have had to experience the unseemly side of sports when his coach was choked and threatened by his teammate during the 1997–98 season. And he wouldn't have had to sweat out the great lockout of 1998.

But seeking out dreams is a strong incentive. And living that dream keeps Todd Fuller pumping iron, practicing his footwork, and driving himself to succeed. The statistics classes can wait. For now, "I would like to play basketball as long as possible," Fuller says.

One incident that occurred during his rookie year helped Fuller understand how very much he appreciated what he had in the opportunity to play in the NBA.

"Mark Price was a teammate of mine," Fuller says. "We had just lost a game at Boston, and Boston was really bad. It was a game we should have won. We played horrible, and the whole mood of the game was down. Mark had gotten two technical fouls and had gotten kicked out of the game. I don't think I played that game—it was one of seven games I didn't play that year. Everybody was kind of in a sour mood.

"We flew on to Philadelphia that night after the game because we were scheduled to play the 76ers the next day. In Philly, Mark and I went down the street to a cafe to get something to eat. It was about twelve at night. After we ate, we were coming back, and we were talking about the game against the Celtics and how things were at the time—pretty bad.

"We came back to the hotel; there was a custodian cleaning the floor at one-thirty in the morning.

"Mark looked at me and he said, 'I don't care how bad things get; you really have to realize the blessings we have to be able to play the game of basketball for a living and have that as a platform for our faith.' I looked at that custodian having to clean the floor at one-thirty in the morning, and I knew Mark was right. It put everything into perspective."

The statistics may not always be exactly what Todd Fuller wants them to be on the basketball floor, but one thing is sure. He's glad to be numbered among the few who ever get to play in the NBA. It really is a dream come true for him.

Q & A WITH TODD FULLER

Q: *What do you like to do to grow spiritually?*
Todd: I like anything that can pull me closer to the Lord. I think the best thing is being in a good Bible study and spending time in the Word. Also, I like hearing a good sermon that is direct and to the point. One that doesn't try to coat over any of the issues in the Bible.

Q: *What are some books you've read that have influenced you in your faith?*
Todd: During the lockout I read *The Silence of Adam*. Also, A. C. Green's book *Victory* is a good one. I read *I Kissed Dating Goodbye* by Joshua Harris. I'm not saying, "I kissed dating goodbye" or that I endorse the whole concept, but it gave me some things to think about. Also, the *Left Behind* series by Jerry Jenkins and Tim LaHaye.

Q: *What was Bobby Jones like as a coach?*
Todd: He maintained sensitivity and humility at the same time. That's a fine line to work with. Some coaches are too laid-back or too aggressive. Coach Jones knows how to push his players without being aggressive.

Q: *How does your faith affect how you play the game?*
Todd: When you get on the floor, it's just basketball. It's just reacting. I do feel that as a Christian you have to approach the game with intensity. Like it says in Corinthians, you mistreat your body to improve it in the long run. That applies to basketball as a believer; you have to, as a Christian on the court, play hard, play intense. Doing those things that will honor and glorify Christ.

Q: *What kind of ministries do you like to be involved in?*

Todd: During the lockout, I played for the Athletes in Action basketball team. Also, I've played in a game Charlie Ward sponsors as an outreach. I like to speak in sports camps and schools. Also, I've done some coaching with Bobby Jones at my old high school. I feel working with kids is a real ministry.

NBA ROAD

1996: Selected by the Golden State Warriors as the eleventh pick of the NBA draft

1999: Traded by Golden State to the Utah Jazz on February 4, 1999

THE FULLER FILE

Collegiate Record
College: North Carolina State

Season	Team	G	FGM	FGA	Pct.	FTM	FTA	Pct.	Reb.	Ast.	Points	Avg.
92–93	NCS	27	53	116	.457	34	44	.773	97	6	141	5.2
93–94	NCS	30	144	299	.482	67	89	.753	253	33	355	11.8
94–95	NCS	27	164	316	.519	116	138	.841	229	35	440	16.3
95–96	NCS	31	225	445	.506	183	229	.799	308	39	649	20.9
Totals		**115**	**586**	**1176**	**.498**	**400**	**500**	**.800**	**887**	**113**	**1585**	**13.8**

Three-point field goals: 1992–93: 1-2 (.500); 1993–94: 0-4; 1994–95: 0-6; 1995–96: 16-43 (.372). **Totals** 17-55 (.309).

NBA Record (Regular Season)

Season	Team	G	FGM	FGA	Pct.	FTM	FTA	Pct.	Reb.	Ast.	Points	Avg.
96–97	GS	75	114	266	.429	76	110	.691	249	24	304	4.1
97–98	GS	57	86	205	.420	55	80	.688	196	10	227	4.0
1999	Utah	42	56	124	.452	30	50	.600	101	6	142	3.4
Totals		**174**	**256**	**595**	**.430**	**161**	**240**	**.671**	**349**	**40**	**673**	**3.9**

Three-point field goals: 1996–97: 0-0; 1997–98: 0-4; 1999: 0-0. **Totals** 0-4.

Hersey Hawkins
Settled in Seattle

VITAL STATISTICS

Hersey R. Hawkins Jr.
Born: September 19, 1966, in Chicago, Illinois
6 feet 3, 200 pounds
College: Bradley University (Peoria, Illinois)
Position: Guard
Family: Wife, Jennifer; children, Brandon, Corey, and Devon

CAREER HONORS

- Received NBA Sportsmanship Award (1999)
- Ranked fifth in NBA in free-throw percentage, .902 (1999)
- Through the 1999 season had the secondlongest run of consecutive games played (511)
- Selected to the NBA All-Star team(1991)
- Named to NBA All-Rookie first team (1989)
- Elected 1988 College Basketball Player of the Year; member of U.S. Olympic team

NOT-SO-VITAL STUFF

- Childhood hero was Julius Erving
- In 1996, he scored the NBA's 7 millionth point

FAVORITE VERSE

"What good will it be for a man if he gains the whole world, yet forfeits his soul?" (Matthew 16:26).

Hersey Hawkins

Seattle, Washington—the Emerald City. Surrounded by water and ringed by majestic mountains, it glistens in the Pacific Northwest sun. Mt. Rainier is within sight on a clear day. Lake Washington provides watersports opportunities. So does the Puget Sound. Ken Griffey lives there, and nearby Bill Gates earns his bazillions. The Space Needle juts into the sky. Famous markets dot the waterfront.

But it wasn't too long ago that Hersey and Jennifer Hawkins were wondering why they had been sent there.

On June 27, 1995, to be exact, the Hawkins family learned that Dad's company would be transferring him any day to faraway Seattle. They would have to leave their green, warm, friendly state of North Carolina for cloudy, rainy Washington.

Hersey's job, of course, was making baskets for his company, the National Basketball Association. His new boss in the Seattle branch office would be a fiery guy named George Karl, and his coworkers were a motley group. There was one guy they called Rainman. Another, they called the Glove.

For his part, Hersey had been perfectly happy working in Charlotte. Oh, he had experienced a bit of a struggle with management, which had not allowed him to make as many baskets as he wanted. In fact, his daily output of attempts had been reduced from an average of 14 when he had worked up north in Philadelphia to around 9 in Charlotte. And as everyone who knows about piecework understands, you get less pay if you produce fewer baskets.

But other than that, he was happy. And observers noticed that his teammates and he were now among the up-and-coming groups of basket makers, and the future looked good. Besides that, Hersey and Jennifer were getting comfortable with the Charlotte community, where they had been for two years. "We had made some good friends there, and we had established some relationships," he recalls.

But then came the news of the transfer, and the Hawkins family felt their future was, well, cloudy.

"When we first got to Seattle," Hersey says now, "we were not very happy. One of the first things you hear about Seattle is all the rain and the cloudiness. So right away, we had a bad impression of the place—before we even got here."

As anyone who has kept up at all on the NBA and the plight of Hersey Hawkins after his trade to Seattle knows, things really have worked out well for him. The veteran guard readily admits Seattle has brought some of his brightest moments in basketball, and for his family it has brought some great opportunities.

So, no, this isn't the story of a disgruntled basketball player who gripes all the way to the bank. It's the story of an easygoing, contented star who, despite a bit of uneasiness at first, has his priorities in the right place. Today he remains grateful for the mysterious ways God directs his life.

When the Seattle Supersonics went after Hersey Hawkins, they were going after one of the final pieces of the puzzle that they felt, when put together, would bring them their first NBA crown since 1979. The Sonics already had the Rainman, Shawn Kemp; the Glove, Gary Payton; plus Detlef Schrempf, Sam Perkins, and Nate McMillan. What they needed was another outside threat at guard. When Karl picked up Hawkins, he said, "We're looking at him to be a 15- to 20-point scorer for us." Hawkins delivered by scoring almost 16 points a game during his first year in Seattle.

Also, the Sonics saw Hawkins as someone who could play

defense. Hawkins's sticky hands (he led the Hornets in steals in 1994–95 with 122) would come in handy in the Sonics' trapping defense. Those hands delivered for the Sonics as well, swiping the ball an average of 152 times in each of his first three years.

But Seattle management signed Hawkins for another reason in 1995: In Hersey Hawkins, they were getting a model citizen.

"He's a high integrity person who cares about his game and cares about his teammates," Karl said at the time. "I think our team is going to gain by his professionalism."

With the addition of Hawkins to an already stellar lineup, some experts thought the 1995–96 season would be the year of the Sonics. They were right. During the regular season, Seattle swept through the competition like a Puget Sound ferry cuts through an early morning fog. They cruised to the top of the Pacific Conference with a remarkable 64–18 record, the best mark in team history. Included in those 64 wins were two wins in three games against the Chicago Bulls, who would post a remarkable 72 wins during the season and whom the Sonics would meet again during the play-offs.

In the play-offs, Seattle breezed past Sacramento 3 games to 1, swept the Houston Rockets 4–0, and held off the Jazz by beating them 90–86 in the seventh game of the Western Conference finals. Then came the Bulls. The Bulls had charged through the Eastern Conference with an 11–1 mark and were well-rested when they hosted the Supersonics in the first game of the NBA championship at the United Center—the house that Michael Jordan built—on June 5, 1996.

For Hawkins, it would be the most incredible experience of his career. He calls playing in the NBA Finals "one of my biggest moments in basketball."

One reason was that the championship series was taking place in his hometown. A graduate of Westinghouse Vocational High School in Chicago, Hawkins had already won a championship in the Second City: the city league championship as a sophomore. He was named Chicago's best high school basketball player as a senior. Now he would try to win a championship *against* a Chicago team.

Imagine the emotion, the rush it must create. A packed house at the United Center, creating enough noise to make Dennis Rodman's tattoos have goose bumps. The laser light show. And the announcer's rolling introduction of the teams.

Hersey recalls how he felt. "As a child, that's what you dream of. Being in the spotlight, having the whole world watching you play. Just these two teams. Playing for the world championship.

"Then you hear your name called in the starting lineup," he says, recalling the wonder of it all.

"To be back there in Chicago, playing in the Finals in front of friends and family. . . . It couldn't have gone any better. It was storybook. The only thing we had to do," Hersey says, qualifying his statement, "was win."

"But Michael spoiled it," he recalls, adding a refrain five other teams sang when they faced the Bulls in the Finals. The Bulls won the 1996 NBA title by beating the Sonics 4 games to 2.

Losing that title round is something Hawkins still thinks about. "It weighs heavy on you when you get that close and then you lose. I think one of the first things you do as a competitor is you sort of . . . ponder, 'What could [I] have done more of, or what did [I] do to make sure [we] won?'

"I guess after we got there the first time, we thought, 'Well, we got there once; it'll be easy to get back there again.' But I think we've had to learn that once you get there, everyone is gunning for you. Everybody is playing their best basketball against you, and you've got to play even harder. You're going to have to be even more focused the next year and the next year. Unfortunately, we haven't been able to even get back to the conference finals, to get a shot at the NBA Finals."

While Michael may have spoiled Hersey's and the other Sonics' dream, nothing seems to be spoiling the enjoyment Hersey and Jennifer Hawkins learned to feel in the rainy city they at first didn't like. Although nothing is certain in the world of the NBA, Hersey says that they like Seattle so much they may make it their permanent home after his playing days are over.

So what changed their mind? Was it that successful first

season in which Hersey played the most minutes he had played since leaving Philadelphia in 1993? Or was it things that happened outside of Seattle's Key Arena?

One answer is the people of Seattle. "Right from the beginning," Hawkins says, "people received me and my family great in this city." One of the most important sources of those people is in the church the Hawkins have found to be their home for worship and service.

"Finding a good church was a key," he says. "We looked for probably a year trying to find the right place. We visited a lot of different churches. One day, the chaplain for the Portland Trail Blazers, Al Egg, told me to visit a church called Antioch, where a fellow by the name of Ken Hutcherson is pastor. He's a former pro football player. We went there, and from day one, we knew it was the place for us."

For many pro athletes, finding a church is not priority one when staking out a new city. But for the Hawkins' and their three sons, the church is an integral part of their life because of a change in Hersey's life that took place when he was in Philadelphia, playing for the 76ers.

While there, he struck up a friendship with the Sixers chaplain, Bruce McDonald. During Hersey's rookie year, Bruce told him about the gospel and asked him to consider trusting Christ as Savior. Hawkins was not ready to make that decision, but McDonald stayed in close contact with Hersey.

Although Hawkins was enjoying a great degree of success in Philadelphia, he struggled to understand and cope with the negatives that come with the high-pressure life of the NBA. Even though he made the NBA All-Rookie team in his first year, he ended the season on a sour note that left him contemplating his place in the league. The New York Knicks swept the Sixers in three games, and Hawkins shot "something like 3 for 27 or 28 from the field. It was awful. I was something like 1 for 9, 2 for 10, for three games."

"I've never really doubted my ability to play in the league, but that was one of the few times when I really seriously thought that I wasn't good enough to play in the NBA. I had to live with that all summer. And of course, people only remember your last game. But in my case they remembered my last three games—when we were swept and I played terrible." And as Hawkins notes about the 76er fans, "Philadelphia can be brutal when you're playing there. I had the coaches and the owners doubting if I could step up my game or if I could be competitive enough to play in the league. So it was a long summer."

Hawkins worked hard at his game during that summer, "probably more . . . than in any summer since I came into the league." Still, Hawkins was ill equipped at that time in his career. He had married his high school sweetheart, Jennifer, during his Philadelphia stay, and he continued to be a high-scoring guard for the Sixers. But he realized he wasn't happy. All the while, Bruce encouraged him, told him he was praying for him, and remained his friend. Jennifer, who had trusted Christ herself, kept up a strong witness at home. For his part, Hersey could not find the key to contentment. He was letting the game eat him up. He would bring it home. He would dwell on it. He would worry.

Finally, in his fourth year with the Sixers, he realized that there was truth to the verse he had heard from Bruce. Jesus answered, 'I am the way and the truth and the life. No one comes to the Father except through me'" (John 14:6). Hersey trusted Jesus Christ as Savior.

By the time the family moved to Seattle four years later, finding a church home was as important as any decision the newcomers could make.

"It's not often that you find a church that you really feel comfortable with and where you like the people as much as we do the people at our church. We've become good friends with the pastor and his family."

One of the benefits of having a former professional athlete as a pastor is that his pastor is not intimidated by having Hersey in the congregation. In fact, Hawkins says that Pastor Hutcherson has challenged him to consider some key decisions regarding his future after basketball.

"I don't know if God's going to call me into a ministry of some sort, because Hutch has made a couple of comments that I didn't happen to come to his church by accident."

One of the ways Hawkins began to show leadership in spiritual matters was by becoming the Supersonics' team chapel leader, which gives him "the responsibility of being the spiritual leader on our team—setting up Bible studies and making sure guys are accountable who are Christians. I think that is a big step for me."

For Hawkins, one of the best times for spiritual rejuvenation came during the lockout of 1998. "I think now more than ever, maybe because of the lockout, spiritually I've started to mature. I've had time to get a lot more involved in church activities."

Several opportunities came to him that either showed his heart for the needs of the unsaved or helped remind him of the importance of his home team: Jennifer, Brandon, Corey, and Devon.

One lesson he had time to learn during the extra time between the end of the 1998 season and the beginning of the 1999 season was one a lot of husbands struggle with: "how to treat my wife" and "how to be a good husband."

"I think during the lockout it was an advantage to be able to spend extra time with my wife. I've really learned what I need to do more to please her and how I need to treat her. We've had an opportunity to communicate more now, and I've had the opportunity to get the frustrations out about some of the things that she doesn't like. . . . I think God has put it on my heart to treat my wife better. And treat her like God tells me, like God treats the church [Ephesians 5:25]." Laughing his easy laugh, Hersey adds, "She's quick to bring up that verse."

If that's not enough to kill the stereotype of a premier athlete, then Hersey's next statement is sure to do so. As the NBA lockout ended and Hawkins prepared for the short training camp to begin, he admitted, "Jennifer has domesticated me. I've done laundry. I clean the house. I do things I've never done before. Now I truly appreciate what my wife does after having to have to do it for a while and help her out."

Besides running the vacuum, another activity that the lockout gave Hawkins some extra time to get involved with was ministry outreach. Specifically, he used some of his time being a part of Jammin' Against the Darkness, an evangelistic outreach in Washington, D.C. Earlier he had participated in a Jammin' in Seattle.

"When I met Steve Jamison about three years ago, he pitched the idea to me and what it was all about. I was excited. I don't think young people get to hear enough about what athletes are spiritually. Kids think we are all about basketball, and I think for us to share another side of us—to let them see that there's a spiritual side and let them see that basketball is not the only thing, that we believe in God—I think that will have a good impression on their life. That's why I do Jammin'."

At the D.C. event, Hawkins was one of the key presenters of the gospel, speaking just before evangelist Jamison preached. For Hawkins, it was a chance to tell the MCI Center crowd his "Philadelphia Story"—the details of why he gave his life to Jesus Christ. Key to his plea for the listeners to turn to Christ was this:

"I would look at myself in the mirror and say, 'Why am I not happy?' After I gave my life to the Lord, I've had the best six years of my life. I look in the mirror now and I know what my purpose is in this life. I'm supposed to go out and spread His Word. That's why I'm here."

It seemed that talking about his faith was becoming increasingly important to Hersey.

When he got back home to Seattle, Hawkins had some time to think about the lockout and the effect it would have on the future of NBA basketball. Hawkins's view of this important topic is related to the way he thinks many people look at pro basketball players.

"I wish everyone could see all the hard work that goes into the game. I think everybody thinks we step onto the basketball floor, play games, get paid a lot of money, and our lives are so easy. They don't understand that there's a lot of preparation that goes into it. They don't understand that when we go home, we are real people with a real life. We have to take out the garbage. Our kids disobey us, and we have to discipline them."

Hawkins is not complaining, just stating what he thinks

people think about NBA players. And because they think this way, it's much harder to win back their affections when there's a situation like the lockout.

"So what the NBA players need to do is to reach out to the fans and tell them that they are appreciated. If that means going out more in public and doing appearances, we need to do that. Every player needs to take it upon himself to humble himself and show people that we appreciate them."

It is clear that Hersey Hawkins has arrived at a good place in his life—and that's not just because of Seattle. He and his family have found a good place to call home, a great place to worship, and important ways to serve God.

Q & A WITH HERSEY HAWKINS

Q: *Does your faith help you when you are going through the frustrations of life in the NBA?*
Hersey: It does. Being a Christian has a lot to do with how you perceive things. When I go through slumps, for instance, I understand that I still must put my faith in God. The fact that you're going to go through some hard times shouldn't be a surprise. You still must carry yourself in a Christian manner, and you go out and play and you don't get frustrated. . . . My faith has definitely had a lot to do with the way I handle trouble. I'm more relaxed. I'm more comfortable with myself, and I'm more at peace.

Q: *Why is your favorite verse Matthew 16:26: "What good will it be for a man if he gains the whole world, yet forteits his soul?"*
Hersey: For some reason, that has always been my favorite verse; I think because of the profession I'm in. I think people perceive that that's all we want: money. But money does not give you happiness; money does not give you peace. If you live your life thinking that way, then you're going to be miserable.

Q: *Are you able to leave the game at the arena?*
Hersey: After my first three years, I finally learned that it's a bad way to live your life if you go home with what you did in the

game. My wife doesn't go to all of our games anymore—she used to go to all the home games. Now, I'll come in and she'll say, "How you doing," and I'll say, "We won" or "We lost," and that will be it. Then the conversation will get on to the kids: "How were the kids tonight?" I think when you mature, you realize that basketball is not the only thing. You start to show the people around you that you appreciate them.

Q: *What do you and Jennifer do to stay strong spiritually?*
Hersey: We have a Bible study that my wife and I do together with one of the chaplains of our team, Jay Holly and his wife. We've been taking a class every Wednesday night just to learn more about the church and the Word.

We try to read daily. One of my goals in 1999 was to read the whole Bible from start to finish, which is something I've never done. I want to start from the beginning and read it all the way through.

Also, I do devotions with my boys every night. That's something that I enjoy, and it's helping me also. We read the Bible, then we read a little story, and then answer questions, and that has been fun.

NBA ROAD

1988: Selected by the Los Angeles Clippers with the sixth pick of the NBA draft

June 28, 1988: Traded by the Clippers with their 1989 first-round pick to the Philadelphia 76ers for draft rights to Charles Smith

September 3, 1993: Traded by the 76ers to the Charlotte Hornets for Dana Barros, Sidney Green, and draft rights to Greg Graham

June 27, 1995: Traded by the Hornets to the Seattle Sonics with David Wingate for Kendall Gill

THE HAWKINS FILE

Collegiate Record
College: Bradley University

Season	Team	G	FGM	FGA	Pct.	FTM	FTA	Pct.	Reb.	Ast.	Points	Avg.
84–85	BU	30	179	308	.581	81	105	.771	182	82	439	14.6
85–86	BU	35	250	461	.542	156	203	.768	200	104	656	18.7
86–87	BU	29	294	553	.533	169	213	.793	195	103	788	27.2
87–88	BU	31	377	720	.524	284	335	.848	241	111	1125	36.3
Totals		**125**	**1100**	**2041**	**.539**	**690**	**856**	**.806**	**818**	**400**	**3008**	**24.1**

Three-point field goals: 1986–87: 31-108 (.287); 1987–88: 87-221 (.394). **Totals:** 118-329 (.359).

NBA Record (Regular Season)

Season	Team	G	FGM	FGA	Pct.	FTM	FTA	Pct.	Reb.	Ast.	Points	Avg.
88–89	PHI	79	441	971	.455	241	290	.831	225	239	1196	15.1
89–90	PHI	82	522	1136	.460	387	436	.888	304	261	1515	18.5
90–91	PHI	80	590	1251	.472	479	550	.871	310	299	1767	22.1
91–92	PHI	81	521	1127	.462	403	461	.874	271	248	1536	19.0
92–93	PHI	81	551	1172	.470	419	487	.860	346	317	1643	20.3
93–94	CHA	82	395	859	.460	312	362	.862	377	216	1180	14.4
94–95	CHA	82	390	809	.482	261	301	.867	314	262	1172	14.3
95–96	SEA	82	443	936	.473	249	285	.874	297	218	1281	15.6
96–97	SEA	82	369	795	.464	258	295	.875	320	250	1139	13.9
97–98	SEA	82	280	636	.440	177	204	.868	334	221	862	10.5
1999	SEA	50	171	408	.419	119	132	.902	200	125	516	10.3
Totals		**863**	**4674**	**10100**	**.463**	**3305**	**3803**	**.869**	**3299**	**2654**	**13807**	**16.0**

Three-point field goals: 1988–89: 71-166 (.428); 1989–90: 84-200 (.420); 1990–91: 108-270 (.400); 1991–92: 91-229 (.397); 1992–93: 122-307 (.397); 1993–94: 78-235 (.332); 1994–95: 131-298 (.440); 1995–96: 146-380 (.384); 1996–97: 143-355 (.403); 1997–98: 125-301 (.415); 1999: 55-180 (.306). **Totals:** 1154-2921 (.395).

Andrew Lang
Worth Noticing

VITAL STATISTICS

Andrew Charles Lang Jr.
Born: June 28, 1966, in Pine Bluff, Arkansas
6 feet 11, 270 pounds
College: University of Arkansas
Position: Center
Family: Wife, Bronwyn; children, Andrew III, "Trey," Alexander

CAREER HONORS

- Blocked his 1,000th Career shot on April 14, 1996
- Scored career high 29 points on January 2, 1996
- Led Atlanta Hawks in blocked shots (144 in 1995)
- Set the Arkansas all-time record for blocked shots; named to All-Southwest Conference team (1988)

NOT-SO-VITAL STUFF

- Friends call him "Drew"
- His favorite food is fish
- Likes to watch the Dallas Cowboys

FAVORITE VERSE

"I can do everything through him [Christ] who gives me strength" (Philippians 4:13).

Andrew Lang

A ndrew Lang is one of those NBA players you don't hear much about. You don't hear about him scoring 35 points and carrying his team through the play-offs. You won't hear about him making his fifth straight All-Star team. You don't—and won't—hear about him winning the slam dunk championship during All-Star weekend.

On the other hand, you don't hear about him in the way you continually hear about players who roll their Range Rovers at 3:00 A.M. or get picked up for driving 110 miles an hour. You don't hear about him in the way you keep hearing about players who complain because their five million dollars are lonely for another five mil to keep them company.

No, you probably don't hear much about Andrew Lang.

But you should.

If you've been fortunate enough to be a Phoenix Suns or Atlanta Hawks or Milwaukee Bucks or Chicago Bulls fan during his stints with those clubs, you would know that, although Andrew Lang is not a basketball name like a Scottie Pippen or David Robinson, he is perhaps one of the best men in the NBA—*best* in the best sense of the word.

Andrew Lang learned long ago that there is a correct way to treat people, a correct way to carry himself, a correct way to speak to others, and a correct way to live his life. And he has spent more than a decade in the NBA conducting himself in a manner that should be bottled by the league and distributed to every strutting, ego-bloated newcomer who signs a fat contract and laces on his "Your Name Here" sneakers.

So, if you haven't heard much about Andrew Lang, it's time you got the inside stuff on the big guy from Pine Bluff, Arkansas. You'll like what you hear.

Let's start back there in Pine Bluff, where Andrew grew up with his sister and his parents. It was there that he was first taught the one thing that has directed his life and guided his steps on a path to respectability. "My parents taught me a fear and a love for the Lord," he says with gratitude.

His mother also taught something else: Sunday school. At the King's Highway Missionary Baptist Church, Mrs. Lang was a regular teacher of Andrew's class. "She taught most of my Sunday school classes," he says. "Whenever I moved up in age, there she was." Nothing like keeping close tabs on your son's spiritual progress.

Although Andrew received a steady diet of God's Word and his mother's teaching, he readily admits that no matter how well his parents raised him, the most important part of his life would have been missing if he had been satisfied just to listen. No, he knew he had to take action.

"There is something every believer has to realize," he says. "No matter how loving and nurturing your parents are, you yourself have to accept Christ as your personal Savior." For Andrew that time came when he was a young teenager.

"When I was thirteen, I had my first sleepless night. Quite honestly, I didn't know if I died right then and there whether I would go to heaven or hell. Knowing the background and the foundation that had been laid before me, there was only one clear choice. Until you reach that point in your maturity, you don't understand that.

"We were in Vacation Bible School that week. The next day I went to what is generally a very comfortable setting. It's me and my peers. Usually, when the invitation is given, everyone pretty much stays true to form. Well, on that day, I took the walk down the aisle. That was my time to trust Christ. If I had not done it, who knows where I would be today."

That decision would have some far-reaching implications for Andrew as he walked down another path that lay before him—one that was presented to him by virtue of his size. It was the path that he would take because of basketball.

As a kid growing up in Pine Bluff, Andrew played a variety of sports: baseball, basketball, football. He ran track. But when he was in junior high school, the basketball coach at Dollarway High, Theodus Broughton, began to notice Andrew. "He would say, 'Hello,' and wish me well," Andrew recalls. That started to turn Andrew's attention toward hoops, even though he was still somewhat interested in football.

Two years later, something else happened to Andrew to draw him deeper toward roundball. Playing in local gyms one summer, looking for competition, Andrew noticed a college kid from the University of Arkansas ready to play. The player, U.S. Reed, was also from Pine Bluff and a star player for the Razorbacks. Andrew and his friends were in awe that he was even there.

After Reed saw Andrew play, to the youngster's delight and surprise, Reed noticed him and suggested he come to a Razorbacks summer camp.

"I told him I would ask my mom," Andrew says. Although he had never been to a basketball camp and didn't know the first thing about it, he was excited. After all, not every kid has a big star at the state school asking him to do such a thing.

When Andrew told his mom that U.S. Reed said he should go to camp, she agreed. The next time they played hoops at the gym, he told Reed, who called Mrs. Lang, made sure the paperwork was done, and put Andrew on the road to Fayetteville.

At camp, Andrew did the expected for any high school player: He worked on the fundamental skills. But to his surprise, after the day sessions he was asked to play with some of the Arkansas Razorbacks players. "These were people I had dreamed about and seen on television for years," Andrew says. "I was in tenth grade, and here they were asking me to play against them.

"I got out there and I played hard and I played loose, because I was in dreamland. I left that camp feeling more confident and more grateful than I ever had about the game of basketball. I had never really seen basketball outside my hometown, so to be on that campus at that basketball camp, and better yet to get to play with those guys, it was just a dream."

Andrew was not a kid who was jaded by projections of his own greatness. He was a high school student who was surprised that his ability was leading to such success. He realized now the wisdom of his basketball coach, who had told him, "You have to stop playing football."

He focused on roundball. He already was close to 6 feet 9. "I later finished high school at 6-11. After that sophomore year, suddenly I was beginning to get attention from state papers, things of this nature. I had never experienced anything like that. It was kind of humbling."

He played Amateur Athletic Union (AAU) summer basketball just before his senior year, and his team almost won the national championship. They were the lowest-seeded team, and they almost defeated the host team. "Those experiences early on really solidified my love for the game."

That AAU tournament thrust Lang onto the national basketball scene. Coaches from around the country began getting in touch with him and offering him their world. Things were changing fast.

"All my life, I had been Mrs. Lang's son, a member of the Baptist church, a student at Dollarway High School. Just a good kid. And now I was being portrayed as a high school All-American." In fact, Lang would finish his senior season by being named a McDonald's All-American.

"I pinched myself all the time because I remember what had happened. I was just going over to the workout, and God put me into a situation that I myself could not have predicted or foreseen—being noticed by U.S. Reed. It's a pretty wild story, but that's what happened."

Andrew graduated from Dollarway and took off for Fayetteville, where he played for two legendary Razorback coaches: first, Eddie Sutton, and later Nolan Richardson. The second of those two coaches would suggest a change in Lang's game that would later serve him well in the NBA. Richardson changed him from the offensive weapon that he had become at Dollarway to a defensive master at Arkansas. By the time he had completed his career as a Razorback, he held the school record for blocked shots.

"In high school, I did score well, but we ran an up-tempo kind of game at Arkansas, and we needed to have a defensive presence. All along, I kept working on the offensive part of my game, but I think my main contribution was to protect the basket.

"We employed full-court pressure, applied traps all over the court in a half-court set, and needed a mobile big man."

And they needed a stopper at the end of the press, which is what Lang provided. "It seemed to be my natural, God-given ability, where timing, agility, and aggressiveness were concerned, to be a shot blocker. Although I enjoyed scoring, I seemed to have a bigger impact on the game from the defensive end."

As a senior at Arkansas in 1987–88, Lang was selected to the All-Southwest Conference team on the strength of his shot blocking, his 9.3 ppg average, and his 7.3 rebounds a game. It would be enough to land Lang on the draft list for the upcoming NBA draft.

Before exploring that, though, it's important to mention another Arkansas basketball player: a star hoopster for the woman's basketball team. She would eventually track with Andrew throughout his NBA career: to Phoenix, to Atlanta, to Minneapolis, and beyond. Her name was Bronwyn Wynn.

"She played at Arkansas all my time there," Andrew says of the hoopster who became his wife. "At the time she was there, the Arkansas women were neck and neck with Texas. Arkansas lost to Texas twice by a total of 3 points." But when Texas got the NCAA bid, Arkansas was left out in the cold. So Bronwyn and her teammates went into the postseason NIT and won that tournament. "I was really proud of her," Andrew says.

Bronwyn and Andrew met at Arkansas, and although they shared a lot of gym time, they didn't talk much in the gym. "It was very awkward to see someone you care about in the gym," Andrew says. "You're all sweaty, you're all tired, and you're there to do a job."

But of course they found plenty of time to talk. Eventually, it was time to take her home to Mama. "She was the first girl who had ever come into my house with me," he says. "When I brought her home to meet my parents, I was so nervous."

Obviously, he didn't scare her off with his nerves. They were married on May 28, 1988.

Keep the number 28 in mind. It keeps coming up.

The NBA draft in 1988 was held on June 28, which happened to be Andrew Lang's birthday. Going into the draft, Lang did not know what his draft status was for certain, though there had been projections that he would be among the top five centers.

Andrew became the draft's 28th pick. Number 28 on his birthday, June 28.

No wonder that when he reported to the Phoenix Suns, Lang asked for uniform number 28. He's been wearing it ever since.

If Andrew Lang is anything, he is a very grateful man. You don't talk to him long without hearing him praise God for some aspect of his life. Even in regard to where he was to spend the first four years of his NBA career, he waxes thankful.

"To go to Phoenix enriched my career, and that is a place I'm awfully grateful to have started in."

For one thing, being drafted and playing for Phoenix allowed him to be involved in the play-offs each of his first four years in the league. Although he never made it to the finals with the Suns, he played in 28 play-off games (there's that number again) for them.

Lang is also grateful for the friends he made in Phoenix. One of them, Mark West, remains Lang's best friend in the NBA. Both players were in Phoenix together for four years, and both play the same position. That would seem to mean that instead of being buddies, they could become mortal enemies, vying for supremacy.

But it wasn't like that. Lang explains the relationship. "Very rarely do you have two centers of equal size and weight battling." But, says Lang, the two players were engaged in "honest work. No fights or arguments. I had never experienced that."

Something else was fresh and rare in the desert air. Lang also became close friends with Keith Brown, the Suns' chaplain. "He was one of my most special friends." Brown mentored Lang and helped him continue to grow spiritually while he wore the orange and blue.

Overall, Lang continues to marvel at the great time he had in Phoenix. "It's only now that I'm older that I can appreciate that opportunity to go to Phoenix to spend four years of my life. I thought I was very happy then, but now as I look back, I realize that I could have gone to a different city and a different organization. But by the grace of God, I went there."

Lang's NBA journey would next take a couple of side trips. First, to Philadelphia as a part of the deal that would send Charles Barkley to the Suns. His stay in the city of brotherly love was brief, just one game (at season's end), before he decided to test the free-agent market and head for the Atlanta Hawks, where he would play for two and a half seasons. During his third season in Atlanta, Lang blossomed, playing some of the best basketball of his career.

Under Lenny Wilkens, Andrew averaged 6.5 rebounds a game and nearly 13 points during the first four months of the 1995–96 season. He had played in every game for the Hawks since he arrived in 1993 and now had found a way to contribute offensively after being a defensive expert all those years. And the Hawks were on their way to the play-offs for a third straight year. What could mess this up for the cocaptain of the high-flying Hawks?

How about a surprise midseason trade? That could put a damper on things. Especially a trade to a team that would win only 26 games all season.

That's what happened to Lang. On February 22, 1996, the Hawks sent Andrew and Spud Webb to the Minnesota Timberwolves for Christian Laettner and Sean Rooks. For the next three seasons, Lang would languish on teams with sub-.500 records.

What was Lang's response to this situation? Trust.

"I don't know what each day brings. That's God's business. There are so many things out of our control. Those are the things God oversees."

"Certainly, I would have loved to have stayed my whole career in Atlanta. I had signed there for six years. What I learned from that was that in all things I have to give thanks. Not long after I left that organization, I began to have some physical injuries. It was during those times, when I didn't have the opportunity to play, that all I could do was reflect.

"God allowed me to see all the positives, all the many blessings throughout my life. That in itself was so much to be grateful for."

Did you get that? Here's a guy who was playing the best basketball of his professional career, under contract to a top organization for six years, and then the rug is pulled out from under him. He is shuffled off to a next-to-the-last place team, where he gets hurt. And he's praising God for it.

At the end of the 1995–96 season, Lang was traded by the T-Wolves to the Milwaukee Bucks. Of this move, Lang was characteristically effusive: "I can't tell you how thankful I am for this opportunity." Keying his enthusiasm was going to a team with a strong contingent of Christians: Armen Gilliam, David Wood, and Elliot Perry. "You can't ask for a better core," he said at the time.

When he arrived in Milwaukee, the team did not have a chapel program, though. Soon he and Wood, a journeyman player who likes to see himself as an evangelist to pro basketball, had one going. "It was a tedious process," Lang says. "But many players benefited from those chapel services. That was a blessing."

While a member of the Bucks, Lang saw his playing time being reduced, and after more than a decade in the NBA, he knew it was time to explore his future options.

A good time to do that was during the lockout of 1998.

"That time of reflection during the lockout helped me mature. Knowing that I have one year left on my contract helped me."

In looking ahead, he soon knew what he would do after his playing career ended. He would somehow minister the gospel.

"I applied for a minister's license," he said of the lockout months. "So I'll be ordained. That will be a start of my ministry. I give all the credit for that to my Lord and Savior Jesus Christ."

Not quite sure how his ordination to the ministry will be used after his career, Lang only knows that he is eager to continue what his career has begun for him. "What better reservoir to start my own ministry than the one I've tapped into over the years. I've met hundreds of people, hundreds of believers. By helping them, I'm sure they'll help me in my ministry."

That ministry will wait a little. In January 1999, after the lockout ended, Lang joined the world-champion Chicago Bulls via a trade. Still, Lang has already begun his ministry at home as the father and leader of his three sons. Whether or not his boys may one day display the abilities of their basketball-playing parents, he will offer each the same advice. "I will encourage them to stay as tender and as humble as they possibly can. I'll tell them that if God gives them the ability and the desire to play basketball, then do that.

"I would tell my boys the same thing any Christian father would tell his son or daughter going out into this big, old, mean world. He that is in you is greater than he that is in the world. Don't ever forget that."

That sounds like a good first message for the new minister when it comes time for him to hang up that number 28 shirt. He will have earned the right to be heard because of a lifetime of dedication to God, a career of honor and hard work, and a heart that is soft toward people and their needs.

Perhaps you hadn't heard much about Andrew Lang before now. But he hasn't toiled in the NBA for all those years for no reason. He's been getting ready for a post-NBA life that will undoubtedly be marked by endless opportunities to serve others. And one that will surely be worth noticing.

Q: *You said Philippians 4:13 is one of your favorite verses. Is it the favorite?*
Andrew: There are so many [great verses]! When you pick that Book up they all jump out at you at different points in your life. The Bible is such a dense and perfect work that when you pick it up and you go to the Psalms and you see the writings of David, or you go to Revelation and you see the things that are to come, it's mind-boggling how it can all be in one book. Everything's in there. As I read daily, I just marvel at the Book.

Q: *You are a student of the Bible. Who is one of your favorite Bible characters?*
Andrew: Abraham, simply because of his relationship with the Lord. At one time they were so intimate. When the Lord visited Abraham, He told him that Sarah would have a child. This was a physical visit. . . . When the Lord came to Abraham and told him of His plans to destroy Sodom and Gomorrah, Abraham actually asked God not to do that. What a relationship! It's not just one Scripture. It's the relationship. To be in the body of Christ is the relationship.

Q: *What keeps you going during the tough times in sports and life, during the frustrating times?*
Andrew: My faith keeps me going. . . . Even though you cannot see God's plan or understand it, your very steps are ordered. I remind myself that I am called to be His disciple, to be His steward, to be a living witness, and to manage well those things He has given us. In the life of a professional athlete or in the life of anyone, you're going to be faced with some things that don't go your way. Only your faith in Christ prepares you for that.

Q: *You played for the much-respected coach of Arkansas, Nolan Richardson. Talk about that relationship.*
Andrew: During my tenure there, there was an illness in the family. Rose and Nolan Richardson's daughter, Rene, had been

diagnosed with leukemia. They had an ongoing battle with her health. That was a big burden on Coach Richardson. Rene eventually passed away. I did not get the opportunity to know Coach or Mrs. Richardson as much as I would have liked. They were always encouraging my play, and I was always prayerful and hoping that God would intervene for Rene.

NBA ROAD

1988: Selected by the Phoenix Suns in the second round of the draft

June 17, 1992: Traded by the Suns to the Philadelphia 76ers

September 7, 1993: Signed as a free agent with the Atlanta Hawks

February 22, 1996: Traded by the Hawks to the Minnesota Timberwolves

July 11, 1996: Traded by the T-Wolves to the Milwaukee Bucks

January 23, 1999: Traded to the Chicago Bulls

THE LANG FILE

Collegiate Record
College: University of Arkansas

Season	Team	G	FGM	FGA	Pct.	FTM	FTA	Pct.	Reb.	Ast.	Points	Avg.
84–85	ARK	33	34	84	.405	18	32	.563	67	7	86	2.6
85–86	ARK	26	88	189	.466	37	61	.607	168	13	213	8.2
86–87	ARK	32	102	204	.500	56	87	.644	240	11	260	8.1
87–88	ARK	30	126	239	.527	27	60	.450	218	10	279	9.3
Totals		**121**	**350**	**716**	**.489**	**138**	**240**	**.575**	**693**	**41**	**838**	**6.9**

NBA Record (Regular Season)

Season	Team	G	FGM	FGA	Pct.	FTM	FTA	Pct.	Reb.	Ast.	Points	Avg.
88–89	PHO	62	60	117	.513	39	60	.650	147	9	159	2.6
89–90	PHO	74	97	174	.557	64	98	.653	271	21	258	3.5
90–91	PHO	63	109	189	.577	93	130	.715	303	27	311	4.9
91–92	PHO	81	248	475	.522	126	164	.768	546	43	622	7.7
92–93	PHI	73	149	351	.425	87	114	.763	436	79	386	5.3
93–94	ATL	82	215	458	.469	73	106	.689	313	51	504	6.1
94–95	ATL	82	320	677	.473	152	188	.809	456	72	794	9.7
95–96	A-MN	71	353	790	.447	125	156	.801	455	65	832	11.7
96–97	MIL	52	115	248	.464	44	61	.721	278	25	274	5.3
97–98	MIL	57	54	143	.378	44	57	.772	153	16	152	2.7
1999	CHI	21	32	99	.323	16	23	.696	93	13	80	3.8
Totals		**718**	**1752**	**3721**	**.471**	**863**	**1157**	**.746**	**3451**	**421**	**4372**	**6.1**

Three-point field goals: 1990–91: 0-1; 1991–92: 0-2; 1992–93: 1-5 (.200); 1993–94: 1-4 (.250); 1994–95: 2-3 (.667); 1995–96: 1-5 (.200); 1997–98: 0-1; 1999: 0-0. **Totals:** 5-20 (.250).

Elliot Perry
Appearances Are Deceiving

Elliot Lamonte Perry
Born: March 28, 1969, in Memphis, Tennessee
6 feet, 152 pounds
College: University of Memphis
Position: Guard
Family: Single

CAREER HONORS

- Dished out 1,000th career assist on December 16, 1996
- Came in second as NBA's Most Improved Player (1995)
- Became the only player in Metro Conference history to score 2,000 points and hand out 500 assists in a career (1991)
- Led Metro Conference in scoring (20.8 ppg, 1991)

NOT-SO-VITAL STUFF

- Nickname is "Socks"
- Was a Junior Olympics gymnastics star as a youngster

FAVORITE VERSE

"Trust in the Lord with all your heart and lean not on your own understanding; in all your ways, acknowledge him, and he will make your paths straight" (Proverbs 3:5–6).

Elliot Perry

Most NBA players don't have the luxury of anonymity. And in most cases it's not just because of their exposure by the media. It's because they simply don't look like most of us. They are bigger, faster, stronger. They have a commanding presence because of their height or their bulk or their muscles. You just can't pass an NBA team on the street and think they are a bunch of bankers out for lunch. You know they are some kind of basketball team.

But Elliot Perry is different. He looks like the rest of us. There are junior varsity point guards who are bigger than he is. At 6 feet and a wispy 152 pounds, Perry is built like an accountant, not a basketball player.

Yet as every basketball scout knows, you have to see a player to know what he's made of. And Elliot Perry has proved over and over to surprised observers that inside that non-NBA body beats an NBA heart and an NBA mind.

Perhaps one of the reasons Elliot has had to battle for his position in the land of the giants is because not enough people know what kind of athlete he has always been. Some basketball players have been able to hang around the league simply because they were big. Manute Bol, for instance, was never accused of being a talented athlete. But, as ESPN's Kenny Main would observe with his deadpan delivery, "He's tall." Others have hung around because they could displace people under the basket with their strength and weight. For those people, there was no need to do a background search to find out if they ever excelled at a sport. They were good because they were big.

Elliot Perry is good because he's a good athlete. Elliot played four other sports before settling in with basketball. There was baseball, in which Elliot played first base. There was soccer, in which he played wing. There was football, in which he was a receiver.

And there was gymnastics. Now, that was Elliot's sport. He tried out and made a Junior Olympics team in the floor exercise, and he actually won a couple of gold medals.

None of this was easy for Elliot's mother to orchestrate— what with her job and her desire to take care of her son. So this single mom enlisted Elliot's aunts to help take care of Elliot and get him to all the places he had to go. "Mom had seven sisters and one brother, so everyone helped at some point when I was growing up."

So, while Elliot was making his way through the beginning stages of his sports experiences, he was learning an important lesson about teamwork. And he was storing up memories that today help him in retrospect as he thinks back to how well his mother did in bringing him up. After all, since his dad died just a month after he was born, he understands what she did for him.

"I don't know if when you're young you can appreciate it, but when you look back on it, you see what people do for you. I can see now what my mom was doing and how she came through it and how she provided. We made it! We always had enough, even though we didn't have much. I look back on those days and I cherish them. I thank my mom for what she did."

Of course, Elliot's mom and his aunts weren't the only people who helped him in his pursuit of excellence in sports. Another person who made a huge difference for Elliot was Michael Toney, an older friend from Elliot's neighborhood. He brought a new sport to the youngster's attention, passing a basketball to Elliot and taking the fifth grader everywhere he went, including the playground.

"He was older, so he could get me onto the playground and get me into the games. I just started getting better. He saw that, and he continued to push me and push me."

When Elliot got a taste of basketball, he lost interest in all those other sports. It paid off, because by the time he was in the eighth grade, he no longer needed someone like Michael Toney to get him into the game. He was already good enough for the varsity at Treadwell High School in Memphis. Through some creative scheduling on the part of his coaches, he was able to play for both the "A" team and the "B" team.

So this young athlete, who had caught on so easily in those other sports, was now on the verge of stardom in the sport that he seemed least physically ready for.

"Once I started playing and once I started getting better and better, I began to think I could play with anybody. I sincerely believed that I could go anywhere in the city of Memphis and play."

By the time Elliot was a sophomore, he was starting to get recruiting letters. Small as he was, he was proving to be a player to notice on a national scale. As Perry moved through the recruiting process, he narrowed his choices to four schools: Memphis, North Carolina, Oklahoma, and Kentucky.

Among those schools, Memphis had a clear head start in the Elliot Perry sweepstakes. For one thing, it would be important to Elliot to play somewhere that allowed his mother to be able to watch his games. "She never missed a game from the time I was in the eighth grade," he explains, suggesting that he would want her to be courtside during his college career.

Another advantage Memphis had was its coach, Larry Finch. "Coach Finch got the Memphis job my senior year in high school, and I knew he was a guard-oriented coach. I knew I could come in and play right away," Elliot recalls.

Not only that, the folks at Memphis had been watching Elliot as he came up through the ranks at Treadwell High School, so they knew how good he was. "I had built a relationship with Memphis throughout the years," Perry says.

But Elliot wasn't eager to sign on with the Blue and Gray without scouting out the other options. One school that tried hard to snag the high-scoring guard was North Carolina. In fact, as Elliot tells it, he received one of only two home visits Dean Smith had ever made to a high school player he was planning to recruit. The only other player in whose living room Coach Smith sat, according to Elliot? A skinny kid from Emsley A. Laney High School in Wilmington, North Carolina, Michael Jordan, who would go on to find fame and fortune selling basketball shoes, cologne, movie tickets, and just about anything with the number 23 on it.

Unlike Jordan, Elliot turned Coach Smith down, although he says, "I had a soft spot in my heart for North Carolina."

Also pulling at Perry's heartstrings were Roy Williams at Kansas; assistant coach Mike Mims at Oklahoma; and assistant coach at Kentucky, Dwane Casey. But when all the recruiting spiels were over and Elliot and his mom were alone in their living room trying to figure out what to do, it was Memphis that won the right to give him a college scholarship.

During Perry's time at Memphis, the team was unable to finish any of the four years in the Top 25 in the polls, but Elliot himself was able to establish himself as a star. Two games stand out as highlights of his college career. As a sophomore, Perry and the Tigers faced Louisville, which would go on to finish this particular season ranked twelfth in the country. Pervis Ellison was a senior, and he had already established himself as one of the best players in the land, and the wise Cardinal coach, Denny Crum, would direct the charge.

All Memphis did was to blow into town and score the first 24 points of the game. Imagine how quiet it must have been at Freedom Hall!

Another game Perry recalls fondly was a personal highlight night. On this day, the Tigers were taking on home state rival East Tennessee State from Johnson City. Elliot lit up the scoreboard for 42 points against the Buccaneers. "I think I missed two shots the whole game."

Clearly, Elliot's Memphis experience was an individual success. He averaged 17.5 points over his 126-game career. He was named Metro Conference first team as a senior. And his mom got to see him play. Staying close to home for college was a success on several levels. He graduated from Memphis with a degree in marketing. He got the playing time and opportunity to be noticed as a player. And it left him in a place where he could continue to be influenced by his old friend, Michael Toney.

Toney, of course, was the person who first caused the basketball bug to bite Elliot. But there was more to Toney than a love for hoops. He also was a man who had a heartfelt love for Jesus Christ.

By the time Elliot was in college, Michael was married. He and his wife took it upon themselves to invite Elliot to attend church with them. As a kid, Perry was never much of a consistent churchgoer, even though his mom did try to encourage it. But as a freshman in college, he took the Toneys up on their offer to accompany him to their church. Sunday after Sunday, Elliot would be there. Even when the Toneys could not make it, Perry was there.

"I continued to go to church and continued to go to church," Elliot recalls. Then suddenly, during his sophomore year, something changed. "Everything that the pastor was saying, or when I would read a Bible verse at night, it seemed like it was always talking to me. I believed in God, but I realized that until I developed a relationship with Jesus Christ, it wasn't enough. I really couldn't praise God like He deserved to be praised."

That decision to put his faith in Jesus Christ, he would later say, "was the best decision I made in my life."

So, the college career turned out remarkably well for Elliot Perry: He stayed close to home, blossomed on the basketball court, and his inner life was transformed. Now, though, he would have to impress the people outside Memphis that a skinny, short kid was man enough to handle the rigors of the National Basketball Association. Soon he was to find out that not everyone thought he could do it. He would discover that it can be a cruel world out there if you don't look the part.

Draft day in 1991 was a day of ups and downs for Elliot. With his extended family gathered around him at home in Memphis, he awaited the decisions of the NBA experts. Round one went by, and the Larry Johnsons, the Stacey Augmons, the Dikembe Mutombos, and the Steve Smiths of the college world were snapped up by teams hungry for improvement.

"I didn't know what to expect," Elliot says of his chances. "I didn't know if I was going to get drafted." Even after scoring 2,209 points, dishing out 546 assists, and averaging 33 minutes a game, it was not a lead-pipe cinch that Elliot had earned a look-see in the NBA.

Round two started. One by one, names were taken from the NBA board. Then the phone rang. It was the Detroit Pistons— Joe Dumars' team, Isaiah Thomas' team, and Vinnie Johnson's team. The suit on the other end of the phone told Elliot that the Pistons wanted him and that they were going to draft him.

But before the Motown Bad Boys could take Perry, he was snatched by the Los Angeles Clippers. The trials of Elliot Perry were about to begin.

Perry reported to the Clippers camp eager to go. But ten games into the season, they chopped him from the roster. "That was probably my low point," he says, "because I had never been cut off any team in my life." He would spend two games with the LaCrosse Catbirds in the Continental Basketball Association (CBA), and he would travel to Charlotte for a 40-game tryout with the Hornets. For all his travels and all his travails that season, he would have but 153 points to show for his efforts in two leagues.

The beginning of the next season, 1992–93, was just as frustrating. He signed with the Portland Trail Blazers and spent training camp with them but was cut before the season began. Back to the CBA he went, this time for an entire season of bus rides, second-rate accommodations, and mostly empty arenas.

"I was really just trying to hold things together," he says of his days in the CBA. "I had been in the NBA, so coming down to the CBA you can see a huge difference. You recall all the good things you got in the NBA that you don't get in the CBA. In the NBA, we got $70 a day for food. In the CBA, it was more like $10. The way you travel and where you stay. You have to wash your practice gear. College was better."

But despite the comedown of having to play minor league basketball, Perry was not about to quit. "I never had the feeling that I wouldn't get back. I knew I could play, and I knew it might take a little time. I've always been a player who has been behind the eight ball. Something always seems to put me in jeopardy. But, always, the Lord has allowed me to come out shining. It just takes a little time."

Perry discovered that during his time of minor-league languishing, he needed to have spiritual help. "I found that you still need to surround yourself with good Christian people, wherever you are. You need to read the Bible. When I played in LaCrosse, I roomed with Ben Hamilton. He was a good Christian guy. He had a good attitude and a strong faith. He taught me a lot of things."

Although Elliot tried to stay positive, something else happened in his second pro season that would have made a lesser man give it up, go back to Memphis, and open up an ad agency or something.

After spending some time with LaCrosse, Elliot was traded to the Rochester Renegades. If being in the CBA was bad news for someone who should have been in the NBA, being in Rochester was akin to being told the world was coming to an end. "It was the worst team in CBA history," Elliot says, now able to laugh about it. "We won nine games all season."

For his part, Elliot didn't do all that poorly, averaging 12 points and almost 5 assists a game. It was good enough for the Portland Trail Blazers, who asked Elliot to come back to training camp for another tryout. Unfortunately, it was déjà vu all over again. Only the dates changed, but the result was the same. Again, Elliot was sent packing just before the NBA season was to begin.

Back to the CBA Elliot went, still not ready to give up. This time, he had a friend in Grand Rapids. Bruce Stewart, the coach of the Mackers, liked Elliot and signed him up.

Twenty-eight games into the 1993–94 CBA season, Elliot was summoned by the Phoenix Suns. On January 22, 1994, Perry signed a ten-day contract with Phoenix. He hasn't played another game in the CBA since.

During the remainder of that season, Perry played in 27 games for Phoenix, and he played well enough to earn a careful examination by the team at the 1994–95 training camp.

This camp would be the fight of Elliot's basketball life, and the "fight" led to what he calls the highlight of his career.

"I had my back against the wall at that camp," he explains. Of course, the Suns already had one of the best point guards in the business in fellow Christian Kevin Johnson. Not satisfied, they had also signed Winston Garland, another talented guard, to a guaranteed contract. There were two other point guards in camp, and nobody needs five of them. Things did not look good for a minimum-salary guy like Elliot Perry.

"I was keeping the faith and trusting the Lord to lead me out of it. I really didn't know what was going to happen. When my agent told me about the situation, I told him to book me a ticket there anyway. 'Don't worry about any other teams,' I told him. 'I'm going regardless of what they've got there.'"

What they got was a young man who had worked hard during the off-season to correct a shooting flaw that had NBA people labeling him a guy with a bad shot. And what they got was a player who simply beat out Winston Garland for the backup point guard job. When camp broke for the 1994–95 season, for the first time in three years Elliot Perry was handed an NBA uniform, not a pink slip.

That season was a dream year for Perry. When Kevin Johnson went down with an injury, Perry started 51 games for the Suns. He averaged nearly 10 points a game and finished in the Top 10 in the league in steals.

The man in the non-NBA body played in all 82 games that season. In the off-season, the Suns rewarded Perry with a six-year, multimillion-dollar contract.

Although he was traded to the Milwaukee Bucks in 1996, Perry continued to be an integral part of his team. And he felt the trade to the Bucks came at just the right time. "It was perfect timing. The trade enabled me to play consistently. The Suns had traded for Jason Kidd, they still had Kevin, and they also got Steve Nash, so it was a perfect time for me to go to Milwaukee." Between his breakthrough year and the last season before the lockout, Perry missed just two games out of the possible 326 games he could have played in.

Would anyone say he's not built for basketball now?

While in Phoenix, Elliot had been surrounded by men who shared his beliefs: Johnson, A. C. Green, coach Paul Westphal, and others. When he arrived in Milwaukee, things were even better. "It was really encouraging," he says of the Christian fellowship there. "We started the first chapel service there with Andrew Lang, Armen Gilliam, Michael Curry, and David Wood. We brought a lot of guys in. We continued to invite guys to chapel and to church."

What burns inside a man like Elliot Perry that drives him to succeed when others give up and go away? Part of it is his innate ability, which has been on display since he was a little kid. Part of it is the drive his mom instilled in him through her own example. Part of it is the learning from men like Michael Toney; his high school coach, Garmer Currie; and his college coach, Larry Finch. And part of it is his desire to please God in his actions and life.

You don't have to be a behemoth to succeed in the land of the giants if you have a heart the size of Elliot Perry's.

Q & A WITH ELLIOT PERRY

Q: *Do you have as much appreciation for a nice assist as you do for scoring the basket yourself?*
Elliot: To set up a play and to get someone else to score an easy basket—that is sometimes more rewarding than anything. It's kind of like a double-edged sword. Your team scored the basket but at the same time you were directly in on the play. It's almost like you scored the basket.

Q: *What do you like to do to help yourself spiritually?*
Elliot: I like to read *Our Daily Bread*. Also, one of my best friends, my college roommate, is a pastor. I go to his church. We surround ourselves with good, spiritual people. We talk together about how the Lord brought us through things. We talk about how God can put us through things not only to test

us but to strengthen our faith as well.

Q: *What do you do during the season to get away from the pressures of the NBA?*
Elliot: We like to go bowling. Some of the guys on the team divided up into bowling teams. We go a couple times a week.

Q: *What kinds of ministries do you like to get involved in?*
Elliot: I speak in a lot of different settings: children's events, to teenagers, at sports banquets, father-son and mother-daughter banquets, at churches. I really enjoy giving my testimony because I think kids can really relate to a testimony. They want to hear where you are coming from. They see where you are. They see you playing basketball, but they don't see that you were cut from the team or that you played in the CBA. I can tell them a lot of the things the Lord brought me through. I really like to share my testimony.

NBA ROAD

1991: Selected by the Los Angeles Clippers in the second round of the 1991 NBA draft. Waived by the Clippers on November 25. Signed by the Charlotte Hornets (December 9)

1992–1994: Played 80 games in the Continental Basketball Association

January 22, 1994: Signed by the Phoenix Suns

September 25, 1996: Traded to the Milwaukee Bucks

March 11, 1999: Traded to the New Jersey Nets

THE PERRY FILE

Collegiate Record
College: University of Memphis

Season	Team	G	FGM	FGA	Pct.	FTM	FTA	Pct.	Reb.	Ast.	Points	Avg.
87–88	Mem	32	140	336	.417	87	108	.806	113	130	420	13.1
88–89	Mem	32	202	437	.462	192	234	.821	109	118	620	19.4
89–90	Mem	30	175	419	.418	137	182	.753	110	150	504	16.8
90–91	Mem	32	235	507	.464	146	184	.793	111	148	665	20.8
Totals		**126**	**752**	**1699**	**.443**	**562**	**708**	**.794**	**443**	**546**	**2209**	**17.5**

Three-point field goals: 1987–88: 53-136 (.390); 1988–89: 24-76 (.316); 1989–90: 17-66 (.258); 1990–91: 49-136 (.360). **Totals:** 143-414 (.345).

NBA Record (Regular Season)

Season	Team	G	FGM	FGA	Pct.	FTM	FTA	Pct.	Reb.	Ast.	Points	Avg.
91–92	LA/CH	50	49	129	.380	27	41	.659	39	78	126	2.5
93–94	PHO	27	42	113	.372	21	28	.750	39	125	105	3.9
94–95	PHO	82	306	588	.520	158	195	.810	151	394	795	9.7
95–96	PHO	81	261	549	.475	151	194	.778	136	353	697	8.6
96–97	MIL	82	217	458	.474	79	106	.745	124	247	562	6.9
97–98	MIL	81	241	561	.430	92	109	.844	108	230	591	7.3
1999	M/NJ	35	39	103	.379	10	14	.714	35	20	98	2.8
Totals		**43**	**1155**	**2501**	**.462**	**538**	**687**	**.371**	**631**	**1474**	**2974**	**6.8**

Three-point field goals: 1991–92: 1-7 (.143); 1993–94: 0-3; 1994–95: 25-60 (.417); 1995–96: 24-59 (.407); 1996–97: 49-137 (.358); 1997–98: 17-50 (.340); 1999: 10-24 (.417). **Totals:** 126-340 (.371).

Brent Price
A Shining Light

VITAL STATISTICS

Hartley Brent Price
Born: December 9, 1968, in Shawnee, Oklahoma
6 feet 1, 185 pounds
College: South Carolina and Oklahoma
Position: Guard
Family: Wife, Marcy; daughters, Madison and Savannah

CAREER HONORS

- Ranked 12th in three-point field-goal percentage, .411 (1999)
- Played his first play-off game in 1998
- Set the NBA record by making 13 straight three-pointers (1996)
- Named first-team All–Big Eight (1992)
- Scored 56 points in one game, including an NCAA record 11 three-pointers (1991)

NOT-SO-VITAL STUFF

- Does a great impersonation of Elvis Presley
- Produced a video on shooting during one off-season
- Enjoys singing and has his own CD and tape

FAVORITE VERSE

"Whatever you do, work at it with all your heart, as working for the Lord, not for men" (Colossians 3:23).

Brent Price

After 13 difficult games into the 1999 NBA season, Brent Price made the highlight reels. If anyone deserved recognition, it was Price, who had endured a rough two weeks. Things hadn't been going so well for the brother of former NBA All-Star Mark Price. In fact, all indications were pointing to the possibility that Price and the Houston Rockets may be better off to part ways.

That is why his amazing shot against the Seattle Sonics during a key early-season matchup must have felt so satisfying.

During the two preseason games the Rockets played (following a management lockout that had cancelled 32 games), Price felt certain he had earned at least a shot at some court time. After all, the team had plenty of superstars to go around, with Hakeem Olajuwon, Charles Barkley, and newly acquired Scottie Pippen. At the shooting guard position, Houston was counting on first-round draft pick Michael Dickerson to develop into a fourth superstar. What Houston needed was someone to distribute the ball to the big three and guide Michael in his development, and Price had proved he could do that.

However, when the season began, Rudy Tomjanovich decided to give the starting point guard position to Matt Maloney, a former CBA player who had distinguished himself in his first year in the NBA by making the All-Rookie second team.

To further complicate matters, Rudy T. seemed to be giving the first call off the bench to his exciting, sharpshooting rookie from Valparaiso, Bryce Drew. After the first two games of the season, in which Brent Price never took off his warm-up shirt, the handwriting seemed to be on the locker-room chalkboard.

Then something immeasurably worse happened to Brent. His grandfather, the man whose name—Hartley Price—he shared, died. The funeral back home in Oklahoma was scheduled for a rare NBA off day, and Brent went home to bury his grandpa.

The frenetic 1999 season indeed got off to a horrible start for Brent Price. Yet Price didn't abandon ship. He didn't demand to be traded or sulk at the end of the bench. He continued to be ready to contribute whenever Coach Tomjanovich called his number.

A few games into the season, Maloney suffered a separated shoulder. Because Drew didn't have the NBA experience to take over the starting role just yet, Price suddenly found himself back out on the court, running Houston's potent offense.

Which led to the February 23 game against Seattle and Price's heroics. The Sonics seemed in control of the game on Houston's home court. They were ahead of the Rockets late through the third quarter. A Detlef Schrempf three-pointer had pushed the Sonics ahead 62–60 after Seattle trailed 60–53.

The Rockets then reeled off 6 straight points to regain the lead. It was 66–62, with just seconds left in the quarter. Brent Price took the ball off a Sonic miss, dribbled just across the half-court line, and, as time ticked away, went up to launch a jumper. When he did, a Sonic defender went up with him to get in his way. That's when Price, now committed to the jumper and with no other option, hung in the air, moved his arm to the right to avoid the leaping defender, and wristed his shot at the basket, nearly 50 feet away. The ball sailed toward the hoop in a perfect trajectory and settled into the net as the buzzer was sounding.

The Summit erupted as fans and players alike recognized the importance of tacking three points to their tenuous lead. Later, Paul Westphal, the Sonics head coach, would say, "Price's three really deflated us."

In the fourth quarter, Price continued to shine, as did his backcourt partner that night, Cuttino Mobley, a rookie. Mobley and Price combined for 13 of 14 shooting from the free-throw line, handed out 11 assists, and scored 29 points between them as they, not the vaunted trio of Dream Team players and megamillionaires, pushed and pulled the Rockets to a 98–86 win over the Sonics.

Of his performance, Price said, "I was able to penetrate and get the other guys shots and of course hit a prayer [his three-point buzzer-beater] that changed the momentum around. I was glad I gave us a little spark."

Brent Price is more than a little spark in the NBA. He is a bright light. He is a shining example of how an athlete should live his life in a world that can be less than conducive to high morals, good attitudes, and family values. In a league that has suffered from the irresponsibility of some of its players, Price is a model of consistency and good will.

In some circles, it would seem proper to compare Price's career in the NBA with the career of his older brother, Mark, who retired before the 1999 season. However, as all families know, it's not a good idea to compare siblings. Somebody's going to get cheated in the process.

However, there is a moment in their comparative NBA lives that is important to recall. It occurred, interestingly enough, when both of Denny and Ann Price's younger sons were playing for the same team. During the 1995–96 season, Mark and Brent were members of the Washington Bullets (now the Wizards).

Mark, the All-Star guard with the long history of NBA success, was brought to town to distribute the ball and score. Backing up Mark was Robert Pack, another NBA player with a good track record.

The third point guard was Brent. He was coming off rehabilitation from ligament surgery, and he had missed the entire 1994–95 season. Prior to being injured, he had played about 2,000 minutes in his first two years with the Bullets but started in just 22 games. Now, backing up the backup point guard, Price felt his NBA career slipping away.

"That could have very easily been my last year in this league," he says. "I was the third point guard, and if I didn't get much playing time during the season, who's going to re-sign me?"

Yet in the sometimes ironic world of sports, odd things happen. Things like Mark Price getting hurt and then Robert Pack getting hurt and then Brent Price suddenly moving to the front of the line. About 30 games into the 1995–96 season, Brent was the Bullets' starting point guard. "I finally got my opportunity off other people's injuries," he says with a nervous chuckle as he thinks about this turn of events.

It was the opportunity of a career—one that many players never get. How often do promising players never get the chance to crack the oh-so-tiny starting lineup of an NBA team and never have the spotlight on them long enough to showcase their skills? For Price, the spotlight would shine for 50 games. And Price would use the time to become a shining light.

"God opened the door," he says. "I stepped in and it was amazing to finally—night in and night out—be able to run the show and show everybody what I could do."

He even got a chance to show Michael Jordan.

It was January, and the Chicago Bulls were in town to take on the Bullets. The Bulls had won the previous NBA championship, and they were on their way to another run at the title. Jordan, of course, had long before established himself as perhaps the greatest player in the history of the game.

To him, this was probably just another game in a long season of contests that seemed to all look the same after a while.

To Brent Price, though, this was a watershed event. This was his chance to prove that after two mediocre years and after an entire season of rehab, he belonged in this league. Then the Bullets' starting point guard, he knew from the opening tip-off that it could be a long night. He was being guarded by greatness. Michael, known for his offense, had made the NBA All-Defense First Team for several years.

"Michael was going to be guarding me. It was like being thrown to the wolves," Price recalls, perhaps forgetting that the wolves would have been a lot easier on him than the Bulls.

What happened next would be "future grandchildren story fodder" for any mere mortal who would have to face Michael. Brent Price scored 30 points that night against Michael Jordan. Included in his barrage of long-range bombs were 6 three-point field goals in 6 attempts. Over the next two games, Price would can 7 more in a row, setting an NBA record for consecutive treys with 13.

But it was the 30 points against Jordan that Price remembers. "That was the biggest game and moment of my career," he says. "We lost the game, but for personal performance, that was probably my best showing."

Brent Price is not a braggart, and his recollection of this game does not come from him as it does from someone who is trying to let you know how good he is. Evidence of that is what Price says he tells people about this game. "I joke about it a lot," he says. "I say, I scored 30 points on Michael Jordan and held him to 42."

But that's all that statement is: a joke. For the record, the self-effacing Price did not guard Jordan that night. He was guarding Ron Harper. In fact, someone else played matador to the hard-charging Bull, letting him run up 42 points.

For Price, this set the tone for what would become his best year in the NBA. Through the rest of the season, he averaged 14 points and 6 assists a game as a starter for the Bullets. With each new game, he seemed more confident. "Night in and night out, I knew I was starting and getting consistent minutes. When you're in a situation like that, your confidence level soars. You don't have to worry about making a turnover here or there. You don't have to force a lot of stuff. You can let the game come to you."

Anybody who has ever struggled with second-string status understands the constant threat of being pulled out of the game—the continual looking over the shoulder at the coach, fearful that the bench will soon be your home.

"I had a great time," says Price. "I was in the middle of the action, and it was my show to run at the point [guard position]."

Among the outstanding stats Price compiled during the season was an impressive .462 percentage from three-point

land, hitting 139 of 301 attempts from beyond the arc. He finished sixth in the NBA in three–point shooting percentage. In
addition, he finished fifth in the league in free-throw shooting
with an .874 percentage.

All around the league, people began to notice Brent Price.

Especially the people in Houston. On the lookout for a
guard to distribute the ball to their scorers, Hakeem Olajuwon,
Clyde Drexler, and Charles Barkley, the Rockets coveted an
unselfish point guard with a deadly outside shot. So on July 16,
1996, they inked Price to a seven-year contract.

At the time, Price told reporters for a Houston TV station,
"If ever there was a perfect fit for me as far as a team and a city,
it's Houston. I've waited a long time to play with players of that
caliber. You get to wondering if your time's ever going to come."

Financially, Price's time had certainly come, for the contract made him a rich man. But on the court, he must have felt
as if he couldn't catch a break. Three days into the Rockets
1996–97 training camp the eager guard suffered a freak accident that led to a spiral of events that would severely hamper
his contributions to the team. Charles Barkley fell on Price's
knee, straining it and putting Brent out of commission for a
while.

"That put me out most of preseason," he recalls, "and
then I fought my way back. I probably came back too early."

Determined to get ready for opening day, Price played in
the final two games of the preseason. In the last game, just
before he would open the season at point for the Rockets, he
broke his elbow.

In December, he was finally able to play, and he had begun
to contribute to the team's success. But 20 games after he had
finally gotten clearance to play, he blew out a knee ligament
(his ACL). That ended his less-than-successful first year with
the Rockets.

However, the grand plan the Rockets had for Price when
he came over from Washington was changed in the interim as
he worked to come back from his injury-plagued first year with
the team. In an effort to replace Brent when he was unable to
play, the Rockets picked up sharpshooting Matt Maloney, who

had spent the 1995–96 season with the Grand Rapids Hoops in the Continental Basketball Association. Maloney performed admirably for the Rockets, finishing third on the team in minutes played and averaging almost 10 points a game.

Maloney's success made it difficult for Price, and Brent knew he was under pressure to get back on the court. At the beginning of the 1997–98 season, he attempted to come back before he was quite ready. "I wasn't 100 percent. Training camp was just five months after my surgery, and I was determined I was going to be out there. Anyone who has ever come back from ACL surgery knows it takes a good year and a half. Here I was after six months, trying to play at this level. I was able to get back on the court. At least I was out there, but it wasn't me. It was almost as frustrating as not playing."

With Price still hobbled, Maloney continued to master the starting spot that Price had come to Houston to fill, thus making Brent's second year with the club even more frustrating.

"It seemed like I had reached the pinnacle of my opportunities, and then the injuries began. It was one setback after another. It's been a tough road. When plans don't turn out the way we think they should, it's always frustrating.

"Once you've been out of the rotation, out for injuries, it takes a while to prove yourself again. For my first two years, I was either rehabbing or trying to prove that I'm back. It was challenging mentally and physically."

Price played in 72 games in the 1997–98 season but only started two games. That meant he had been with the team for two seasons going into the 1999 season but had played in just 97 games of the team's 162 regular season games, starting in only two.

That's why Price was excited to begin the lockout-shortened 1999 season in good shape and eager to go. He figured it was finally time to shine. The team was poised to make a run for the title with the addition of Pippen, and Brent felt it was his time to run the show.

But then he began the year with those two frustrating DNP (did not play) coach's decisions next to his name. It was starting to look like Washington all over again.

"You have to work not to get down when others in the organization are down on you," he says. "As a Christian, that's where your faith plays a big part. Mentally, it's a roller-coaster ride—this league. In a regular season, there are so many ups and downs that one day you can play well and the next day you can be on the bench. Mentally, you have to stay focused on your faith. As a Christian I know that God is in control and that His will will be done in my life. That's an aspect that an unbeliever doesn't have.

"I always tell people that I don't think I could play in this league if I wasn't a believer. I would kind of be blowing in the wind. The league is so temporary. You could have an injury at any time or you could have a bad game. You could be traded. So, you're living day by day in this business. Without that constant rock in your life—without Jesus—it would be very difficult."

For Brent Price, what happens on the basketball court is certainly important, and he recognizes the importance of what he is doing in the business he is in. Yet he's so much more than a basketball player.

He's a singer who has produced his own CD/tape titled *A Place Called Hope.* As a youngster growing up in the basketball-playing Price family, he was also known as one of the gospel-singing Price brothers. The family would appear in churches when Brent, Mark, and their brother Matt were growing up—singing southern gospel music. Now both Brent and Mark have recorded their own albums.

"Music has been such a big part of my life," he says. "Basketball is my job, but music is my love. It's just a part of me. I love music—all styles and forms. I can worship so much through music. It's something my parents passed down to me."

Even during the lockout that preceded the 1999 season, Price was able to use that love of music. "Usually, I never get to experience the Christmas season with my family, but I was able to do a lot of singing and speaking during the holidays. It was a lot of fun. I always look for opportunities to sing and share my faith.

"I don't know if my music will lead to anything after I'm

finished playing basketball. It may not. It may just be a hobby, but I'd like to record another album. I've gotten letters about how certain songs have ministered to people. Besides, the songs mean something to me too."

He's an instructor who has put together a videotape that discusses the fine points of shooting a basketball. "That was something a former coach had always dreamed of doing, putting a good shooting video together." Also, Brent's father was a longtime coach, both at the college and the NBA levels, and he had developed his own methods of teaching shooting. Those methods, of course, worked quite well for his two sons, who set shooting records in the NBA, so Brent felt they were worthy of putting into a video. But there was something else he wanted to do.

"I've always wanted to get my dad's principles about shooting on video. But I also wanted to go deeper and get the Christian message in there."

The result is a video with great lessons on shooting, some zany humor, and a clear presentation of the gospel.

He's a grandson, who, in the midst of his struggles to regain his spot in the lineup during the 1999 season, buried his grandfather. The season was barely a week old, and Brent was battling to win his starting position back when he learned that his father's dad had died.

"That was probably the closest person to me that I've lost," he said about his grandpa's death. "We have a very close-knit family."

But with this grandfather, there were two especially important ties: Brent was named after this grandfather, Hartley, and he was born on Grandpa Price's birthday. "Letting go of someone you love puts things into perspective. More than ever in my life, when I look at my wife and my two children and my parents—the people around me—I realize what a short journey we have. I realize that every day God gives you is important and I have to make the most of it for Him.

"As I get a little older and think about the first passing in my family, it just brings to home that we have just a short time. The Bible tells us to make the most of our time. With all of our relationships, not just family and friends, but with teammates, we have to give the message of Christ to a dying world."

And, with a family of his own, *he's a husband* to Marcy, his high school sweetheart, and *a father* to two young daughters, Madison and Savannah. "God has been so good to me," Price says. "He has blessed me beyond measure with things way beyond basketball. Family. Children. The love that I've been able to experience."

With his family, Brent enjoys being part of a church they attend in Houston. "We love to go to church and get involved in our Sunday school class. I love to be in church on Sunday with my church family. We also have an accountability group that meets once a week. Marcy is involved in a Bible study once a week."

The 1999 season was a year of renewal for Brent Price on the basketball court. Finally healthy again and able to display his skills, he moved beyond that key February 23 game and assumed a key role for the Rockets as they made a run at the NBA title. His playing time increased, his scoring became more consistent, and he was finally beginning to fulfill the hopes the Rockets had for him when they signed him three years earlier.

Yet whether he was knocking down threes and dishing off no-look passes to Charles Barkley or whether he was involved in some aspect of his off-the-court life, Brent Price has proved in a number of ways that no matter what kind of contract he signs or no matter what others might expect of him, he remains a shining light.

Q & A WITH BRENT PRICE

Q: *Your favorite verse, Colossians 3:23, is a favorite of many believers. How important is honoring God to you?*
Brent: I have a lot of favorite verses, but [this has] been a life's verse for me, especially since a friend reminded me of that verse in college when I was going through some tough times. People are constantly judging your playing. You've got coaches and the media to contend with. You've got fans calling into radio shows, and there are times when it's easy to get caught

up in that, listening to what men say, and trying to work for the favor of man. As a player, that's one of the worst things you can do. Every night I step on the court, I play for His glory and to honor Him, and I don't worry about man and what they think as long as I'm doing the job God wants me to do.

Q: *Talk about the lifestyle that you as a Christian must endure to play in the NBA.*
Brent: It's a tough lifestyle. I talked to my brother a lot about it. I can't imagine playing in this league if I was not a Christian. Basically, everything the world thinks is success is in the NBA. You've got the money, the women, the material things, and so on. As Christians, we are in the world but not of the world. We are surrounded by such a worldly business. Corruption is around you on a daily basis. I'm talking about people's profanity, the carousing—there are a lot of things going on around you. As you're traveling day in and day out with all this going on around you, it wears you out.

That's why it's so important to get involved in things that are keeping me fed and in the Word of God. I'll go on a long road trip, and by the end of the road trip, I can feel myself beat down a little bit physically and spiritually. It's kind of like garbage in, garbage out when you're around that stuff so much.

Q: *What about the problem of being well known in Houston as a member of the Rockets? Is it tough to go out in public?*
Brent: People know who I am. But I feel that I have the best of both worlds. I can take my wife out to dinner, and people might come up for an autograph or you hear people talking about you. But it doesn't affect my ability to go out into society and do the things we like to do.

Q: *How do you handle situations when you don't get the fair shake you think you deserve from a coach or from the team?*
Brent: The bottom line is that in this life, I'm not necessarily playing for the commissioner, I'm not playing for the coach, I'm not playing for the owner. I'm playing for the glory of God and

where He has placed me. In doing that, I think the other authority figures will be pleased and honored.

NBA ROAD

1992: Selected by the Washington Bullets in the second round
of the NBA Draft

July 16, 1996: Signed with Houston as a free agent

THE PRICE FILE

Collegiate Record

Colleges: University of South Carolina; Oklahoma University

Season	Team	G	FGM	FGA	Pct.	FTM	FTA	Pct.	Reb.	Ast.	Points	Avg.
87–88	SC	29	98	213	.460	66	77	.857	47	78	311	10.7
88–89	SC	30	144	294	.490	76	90	.844	75	128	432	14.4
89–90	Transferred; did not play											
90–91	OK	35	178	428	.416	166	198	.838	127	192	613	17.5
91–92	OK	30	182	391	.465	120	152	.789	111	185	560	18.7
Totals		**124**	**602**	**1326**	**.454**	**428**	**517**	**.828**	**360**	**583**	**1916**	**15.5**

Three-point field goals: 1987–88: 49-112 (.438); 1988–89: 68-139 (.489); 1990–91: 91-244 (.373); 1991–92: 76-194 (.392). **Totals:** 284-689 (.412).

NBA Record (Regular Season)

Season	Team	G	FGM	FGA	Pct.	FTM	FTA	Pct.	Reb.	Ast.	Points	Avg.
92–93	WAS	68	100	279	.358	54	68	.794	103	154	262	3.9
93–94	WAS	65	141	326	.433	68	87	.782	90	213	400	6.2
94–95	WAS	Injured; did not play										
95–96	WAS	81	252	534	.472	161	191	.874	228	416	810	10.0
96–97	HOU	25	44	105	.419	21	21	1.000	29	65	126	5.0
97–98	HOU	72	128	310	.413	98	119	.824	107	192	532	5.5
1999	HOU	40	100	207	.483	46	61	.754	80	112	292	7.3
Totals		**351**	**765**	**1761**	**.434**	**433**	**526**	**.823**	**635**	**1153**	**2296**	**6.5**

Three-point field goals: 1992–93: 8-48 (.167); 1993–94: 50-150 (.333); 1995–96: 139-301 (.462); 1996–97: 17-53 (.321); 1997–98: 73-187 (.390); 1999: 46-112 (.411). **Totals:** 333-851 (.391).

David Robinson
A Strong Foundation

VITAL STATISTICS

David Maurice Robinson
Born: August 6, 1965, in Key West, Florida
7 feet 1 inch, 250 pounds
College: U.S. Naval Academy
Position: Center
Family: Wife: Valerie; children: David Jr., Corey, and Justin

CAREER HONORS

- Named to the NBA 50th Anniversary team of all-time best players (1996)
- Selected NBA All-Star eight times (1990–95, 1996, 1998)
- Named NBA Most Valuable Player (1995)
- Played on three U.S. Olympic basketball teams (1988, 1992, 1996)
- Honored as 1992 NBA Defensive Player of the Year
- Chosen 1990 NBA Rookie of the Year

NOT-SO-VITAL STUFF

- Scored 1,320 on his SAT test in high school
- Loves to spend time on computers
- Enjoys playing the piano

FAVORITE VERSE

"You are the light of the world. A city on a hill cannot be hidden" (Matthew 5:14).

David Robinson

After a decade of playing pro basketball, he has a roomful of awards, a multiyear contract that pays in the $70 million range, an NBA title, and the respect of everyone connected with the game. What else is there to say about David Robinson, a dedicated athlete who graduated from the U.S. Naval Academy as college basketball's player of the year—a muscular, talented, almost unstoppable force on the basketball court—who left school with a number 1 draft selection but honored his final two years of military commitment before joining the NBA?

What else can be said about his Christian testimony, which began when a man on an airplane explained the gospel to him and grew into fruition when another man challenged him that if he was indeed a Christian, he'd better be spending considerable time reading God's Word and talking with His Savior in prayer?

Can anything much be added to an NBA story that sounds like it was created as the plot for a feel-good movie? How he came to the lowly San Antonio Spurs, won the Rookie of the Month Award each month of his first season and turned the franchise into a contender pretty much single-handedly? How he was so good and so much was expected of him that he began to be criticized for being "soft" because he couldn't do what no one else in the league could do either: unseat Michael Jordan and the remarka-Bulls?

So what else is there to say about the man?

Well, one thing is certain. David Robinson has proved that he will put his time and effort where his reputation is in regard to helping others.

While many athletes take their riches and squirrel them away, using them solely on personal pleasure palaces and extravagant living, Robinson has shown an honest concern for the people of his adopted hometown of San Antonio. A look at the work of the David Robinson Foundation (DRF) will show that this man has a heart for others.

David and Valerie Robinson began DRF in 1992. And while many athletes have foundations, and even some Christians have them, not many will boldly declare that their benevolent organization is a "Christian organization with a mission to support programs that address the physical and spiritual needs of the family." Yet the Robinsons use that kind of language openly, not afraid of being associated with their faith in such an open forum.

Among the activities of the DRF are these projects:

- *Robinson's Neighborhood Students.* This is a scholarship and mentoring program that helps nearly one hundred students in San Antonio.
- *Feed My Sheep.* This program provides food to other organizations that specialize in feeding the hungry.
- *The Ruth Project.* This outreach targets young mothers by offering diapers and baby food to needy infants and toddlers. With the David Robinson Foundation providing the resources, other organizations are given the goods to help those in need.

In addition to those major projects, DRF also makes grants to other charitable organizations and helps out fund-raisers in the community by donating tickets, basketballs, and other Spurs and David Robinson–related paraphernalia.

Perhaps the hallmark achievement of the foundation has

been a $5 million donation to establish The Carver Academy. The donation came in the form of a $3 million gift and a $2 million matching grant. The academy is part of the Carver Community Cultural Center (CCCC), which is located in San Antonio's Eastside community, a predominantly African-American part of the city. The CCCC's plan at the time of Robinson's gift in 1997 was to provide that community with a number of positive centers, including a school to prepare students for college through a rigorous education, a new community center, and a neighborhood outreach location.

The gift from DRF provided half of the money the organization needed to fund the ambitious project. Soon the building for the new school was under construction, with officials hoping to have students attending classes by the fall of 2000.

So looking at his foundation is one way to get to know a little more about David Robinson—seeing whom he wants to help and how he does it. Another way, of course, is to listen to the man himself, to let him explain what goes through his mind. After all, a man as intelligent as David Robinson can speak clearly for himself. Take a look at what David says about some important topics: (1) becoming a Christian, (2) learning from God, (3) dealing with temptations, and (4) having worship and fellowship.

ON BECOMING A CHRISTIAN

David Robinson's testimony of faith is a clear call to understand the difference between simply trusting Christ as a way of making sure of heaven and turning a life over completely to him. As David tells the story, it's easy to see what a transformation that distinction has made in his life.

"My mother was a Christian, and she always wanted me to go to church. She went to the Baptist church all the time, and I just always thought it was boring. So, she dragged me to church with my brothers and sisters. She'd get us dressed up and take us. I got to the point when I said, 'Man, when I'm old enough, I'm not going to church anymore—it's just boring.'

"But I grew up around it. I heard the stories and kind of understood a little bit about what the Bible said, but I didn't really get the whole gist of it.

"It's so true what they say about people not being able to give you a relationship with Christ, because you really can't get it from anybody. You have to experience it yourself. The good thing was that I was exposed to it, and my mom was faithful. I think that really paid off.

"Today we use the word 'Christian' so much, and I don't think it has a great connotation for a lot of people. We see a lot of Christians who aren't really strong, so it doesn't really mean as much.

"My problem was that at first I didn't see the need for Jesus. I just didn't see why He was so important and what in the world He could do for me."

That changed during Robinson's return flight from the 1986 World Championships, an amateur competition featuring some of America's top college athletes in international competition. The naval cadet enjoyed the games, and his team won the championship game. Now, though, Robinson wondered what the point was. "Here I am winning the World Championships," he recalls, "and I have to go back to another college basketball season and re-prove myself all over again. I knew something was missing. I didn't know what it was."

On the plane were several evangelists who had been to an international convention. One of them, seated next to David, "talked to me about Jesus. I liked what he said. It still didn't click in my head what he was talking about, but I liked what he said. He asked me if I wanted to pray and receive Jesus. I said, 'Sure!' I prayed with him, but nothing in my life really changed. My heart wasn't ready for it. But it did plant a seed in my mind. I thought, 'There's gotta be more than this. I've gotta find out what it is.'

"It would nag me once in a while, but I still never really read the Bible or tried to understand how my life was supposed to be."

Five years later, as a professional basketball player for the Spurs, Robinson opened his home to a visitor, Austin minister Greg Ball of Champions for Christ. "He wanted to talk with me. I did have some questions. I knew I had to find out more about this

Christian stuff. When I sat down with him, he really challenged me. He asked me, 'Hey, do you love God?' I said, 'Yeah, sure.'

"Then he asked me, 'How much time do you spend reading your Bible and really learning about God?'"

"Well, not often," the basketball player answered.

"How much time do you spend praying?"

"Well, I don't pray that much."

Ball told Robinson how in the Old Testament, God asked the nation of Israel to honor Him one day a week. Then Ball asked, "When was the last time you took one day and praised God?"

"I don't think I ever did that," Robinson admitted.

"Well, when you love someone, don't you want to just spend all your time with that person and honor that person and just really bless that person? That's what love is about, isn't it?"

With that question, Robinson "realized that I didn't love God. You can say all you want, but if your actions don't back up what you're talking about, then it means nothing!"

"It just broke my heart," Robinson recalls. "I realized that day that God had given me so much, and I never thanked Him. I never once just sat down and thanked Him. I could see His love and His passion for me that day.

"My heart broke, and I started crying. I said, 'God, I'm sorry. I realize that You really are real. From now on I want to learn about You, I want to walk with You, I want to know You, I want to just love You.'"

With that commitment, Robinson began reading his Bible and praying regularly. "My whole world opened up because that's when I started finding out that Jesus Christ is the reason we know of God's deep love for us. That's when it really became real to me to walk with God."

LEARNING FROM GOD

David Robinson, of all Christian athletes, is looked upon as one with maturity, with a real sense of mission, and with complete dedication to his faith. But he seems to sense that he hasn't arrived, that he still has much to learn about how to serve God and live for Him.

"The one story that keeps coming to my mind is the story of Moses. When Moses was at his prime—he's forty years old—he's big in the community. . . . He's got all the money and all the power. But God said, 'So what? I can't use you.'

"God waited until he was eighty and stuttering and in the world's eyes pretty useless. That's one thing God has really been dealing with me about: 'Hey, David, I know that right now you're doing well career-wise and everything, and it seems like now is the time to do something just awesome. But you're not ready. I haven't put in you what I want to put in you yet.'

"God has been dealing with me about preparation and patience and going through some trials and developing character. He's saying, 'Learn how to make Me your sufficiency.'"

For David Robinson, the 1999 season brought some surprising changes—and more success. Spurs coach Gregg Popovich decided that his "go-to" guy on offense would be Tim Duncan instead of Robinson. While this left David with fewer scoring opportunities, it freed him to concentrate on rebounding and defense.

The Spurs and Robinson responded well, finishing the season with the best record in the NBA, and entered the playoffs with the home court advantage. In an exciting championship series with the New York Knicks, the Spurs captured the title.

It was another testament to Robinson's maturity as he willingly assumed a lesser offensive role for the good of the team.

For the present, Robinson knows "God wants me to be a good husband now. . . . [a good father, and] a good basketball player, and that's all I know. God's been bringing that story of Moses back to my heart and mind over and over again. It's like God is putting little things here and little things there until the pieces all fit together. Then I can say, 'Wow, this is where He wants me to go.'"

ON TEMPTATIONS

Although most of the major indiscretions and moral failures in the sporting world happen to athletes who have not professed faith in Jesus Christ and do not testify of their love for Him, once in a while a Christian athlete stumbles. When he or she does, it leaves a very deep stain on other athletes who are trying, as David Robinson does, to lead an exemplary life. Robinson understands the element of danger that surrounds his life as a pro athlete, and he tries to prepare himself to avoid the trouble in regard to money and other things that can overtake a person.

"It's hard. It's sort of like fattening the calf for the slaughter. Temptation is so subtle. People look at you and they think, 'Oh, man, your life is so easy and so good.' But you know, there's a lot to be said for simplicity. There's a lot to be said for not having things, because they don't get in the way when you don't have them.

"God keeps working with me, and the one thing God wants us to realize is that He is our everything. He is our sufficiency, and we need to learn to come to Him and trust in Him in every situation. Some days it's easy to think, 'I got it under control today, Lord. Don't worry about it.' But that's not what He wants.

"I've got to minister to my wife and keep my children in line and minister to them. And then I've got to go out and minister to everybody else—while I try to keep my own act together. It's a good challenge. It's a good stretch, and I'm enjoying the challenge. But God's been testing me."

HAVING WORSHIP AND FELLOWSHIP

Imagine how hard it must be for a pro athlete of any kind to find a church home where he can just walk in the door like everyone else, find a seat, and quietly and reverently enjoy the service. The whispers, the stares, the people wanting to get to you can only distract from worship.

Imagine how much harder it must be for a superstar—one everyone recognizes, and one who stands more than 7 feet tall. You can't run and you can't hide. You just have to live with the celebrity and the attention that comes with being an NBA big man.

"It was kind of funny. For a while we were going to different churches to see which church we felt comfortable in and where we felt God was leading us. It seemed like being a celebrity would kind of get in the way a little bit. But now that we're pretty much settled into a church, it's a positive thing. If I go or if I do something, I think it encourages people to do more.

"Attending church is very important. I like small groups, and I like small churches. Small groups can be very good for you.

"I also have fellowship outside of the church. On my team we've had guys who are really strong, and we spend a lot of time praying together and in the Word. When we're out on the road and I can't be in church, it's great because I have good fellowship every day.

"It's important to have support at home, so my pastor and I have a good relationship. We sometimes talk and share and study together. And I know a few guys at church on a good personal level, but not a lot of guys. It's difficult for me to establish those because I don't have as much time to invest in those relationships.

"My church is important to me."

Q & A WITH DAVID ROBINSON

Q: *You've said you read a lot. What kinds of reading do you get the most from?*
David: I read constantly. I enjoy different things. I try not to get myself too busy that I get away from the Word of God. I enjoy other people's perspective on things. There's an awesome book by Howard Hendricks called *Living by the Book*. It's a Bible study helps book. It teaches you how to read the Bible and how to draw the meaning out of the text. I usually don't get into storybooks, but I liked *The Prophet* by Frank Peretti. I get into teaching books and commentaries. I read just about anything you can imagine.

Q: *Why is it so important to you to be vocal about your faith?*
David: It's just a joy that is in my heart. I don't judge other people by the way they witness, because I think the Lord has dif-

ferent parts of the body. He calls different people to do differ-ent things, and I just happen to have a big mouth. I like to talk about my faith. If something is great, I feel I have to share with people. I understand that some people have more of a burden to pray. Or some have more of a burden to do other things, which is fine. I really have a burden to see people's eyes opened and to see them grow in the Lord—not just give their lives to Christ, but to really mature in the Lord.

Q: *How do you balance your professional life with your family life?*
David: I make sure my wife and boys get the significant portion of my time—of my quality time—and that I don't neglect them. You're busy all season, you're playing, and then during the off-season you want to be ministering to people and doing differ-ent things. You have to draw the line somewhere; you have to tell people, "No." You have to make sure you don't neglect your family at home. It doesn't do any good if you're out there preaching about family, and then you come home and your wife tells you she hasn't had enough time with you and that you're neglecting her.

Q: *When you were a kid, did you have dreams of NBA stardom?*
David: There is no way I could have predicted this. Even in my wildest dreams I couldn't have predicted all this. To be honest, I wanted to be a scientist or something. You know, make decent money. I never thought about making a lot of money. I just kind of figured, I want to have a nice solid job and be like my dad: raise a nice little family. I would have been entirely happy with that.

NBA ROAD

1987: Selected by the San Antonio Spurs (first pick in the first round)

1987–89: Served in the military (U.S. Navy)

1989: Reports to San Antonio and a pro basketball career

THE ROBINSON FILE

Collegiate Record
College: The U.S. Naval Academy

Season	Team	G	FGM	FGA	Pct.	FTM	FTA	Pct.	Reb.	Ast.	Points	Avg.
83–84	Navy	28	86	138	.623	42	73	.575	111	6	214	7.6
84–85	Navy	32	302	469	.644	152	243	.626	370	19	756	23.6
85–86	Navy	35	294	484	.607	208	331	.628	455	24	796	22.7
86–87	Navy	32	350	592	.591	202	317	.637	378	33	903	28.2
Totals		**127**	**1032**	**1683**	**.613**	**604**	**964**	**.627**	**1314**	**82**	**2669**	**21.0**

Three-point field goals: 1986–87 1-for-1.

NBA Record (Regular Season)

Season	Team	G	FGM	FGA	Pct.	FTM	FTA	Pct.	Reb.	Ast.	Points	Avg.
89–90	SA	82	690	1300	.531	613	837	.732	983	164	1993	24.3
90–91	SA	82	754	1366	.552	592	777	.762	1063	208	2101	25.6
91–92	SA	68	592	1074	.551	393	561	.701	829	181	1578	23.2
92–93	SA	82	676	1348	.501	561	766	.732	956	301	1916	23.4
93–94	SA	80	840	1658	.506	693	925	.749	855	381	2383	29.8
94–95	SA	81	788	1487	.530	656	847	.775	877	236	2238	27.6
95–96	SA	82	711	1378	.516	626	823	.761	1000	247	2051	25.0
96–97	SA	6	147	72	.500	34	52	.654	51	8	106	17.7
97–98	SA	73	544	1065	.511	485	660	.736	775	199	1574	21.6
1999	SA	49	268	527	.509	293	363	.658	490	103	775	15.8
Totals		**685**	**5899**	**11275**	**.523**	**4892**	**6611**	**.740**	**7881**	**2028**	**16715**	**24.4**

Three-point field goals: 1989–90: 0-2; 1990–91: 1-7 (.143); 1991–92: 1-8 (.125); 1992–93: 3-17 (.176); 1993–94: 10-29 (.345); 1994–95: 6-20 (.300); 1995–96: 3-9 (.333); 1996–97: 0; 1997–98: 1-4 (.250); 1999: 0-1. **Totals:** 25-97 (.258).

Brian Skinner
Quiet Strength

VITAL STATISTICS

Brian Skinner
Born: May 19, 1976, in Temple, Texas
6 feet 10, 255 pounds
College: Baylor University
Position: Forward
Family: Wife, Rebecca

CAREER HONORS

- Received All-American honorable mention (1998)
- Won a gold medal for USA Basketball in the World University Games (1997)
- Played for the gold-medal winning U.S. team in the World Championships (1996)

NOT-SO-VITAL STUFF

- Majored in environmental studies
- Brian's sister, Pamela, also played college basketball

FAVORITE VERSE

"How precious to me are your thoughts, O God! How vast is the sum of them! Were I to count them, they would outnumber the grains of sand" (Psalm 139:17–18).

Brian Skinner

Not long after the NBA lockout ended in January 1999, the Los Angeles Clippers signed a first-round draft pick to a three-year contract. When they did, they bolstered a front line that included three 7-footers and two players just a couple of inches below that mark.

He was a player who didn't go to one of the huge power-house basketball mills. He liked to block shots. And he was not Michael Olowokandi of Pacific University, the so-called Kandi Man. No, the rookie signed to help bring respectability to a franchise that has long suffered from a string of bad seasons was Brian Skinner from Baylor University.

If the name Brian Skinner does not blast its way onto a fan's awareness the way the Kandi Man can, that's perfectly OK with Skinner. For him, playing basketball is not about head-lines and fame. It's about playing hard, earning what people give him to play the game, and having the independence to be his own person.

He found out in high school that he didn't need everyone fawning all over him to make him happy. In an average-sized town (50,000) in Temple, Texas, Skinner was not the typical high school star jock. Sure, at Temple High he was good on the basketball court, or he wouldn't have been recruited by such colleges as Wake Forest, Florida State, Oklahoma, and Boston

College. But his view of things was that he wasn't all that special.

"I was a nerd," he says in a refreshing, self-deprecating way. "Well, maybe not a nerd, exactly, but I was somebody who was quiet. I didn't have a lot of friends. I was more of a loner."

To prove his point, he tells of the night a friend and he decided to skip a big event at the high school. Instead they went fishing. All night. That was unusual, because Brian says that usually he wasn't out at night. "People would ask me why I didn't go out, why I didn't do things. I said there was always something better to do."

On the basketball court, Skinner insists he was not considered that special. "I really wasn't in the limelight. I wasn't a superstar. I guess I was the star behind all the lights and all the glamour. I averaged 19 points and 12 rebounds my senior year, but I didn't get a lot of recognition. I didn't play in a lot of All-Star games as other players did, but it didn't bother me."

In the classroom, Skinner did well in a school noted for its excellence. Between 1989 and 1998, Temple produced ninety National Merit Scholars, and two students from that high school achieved perfect 1600s on their Scholastic Aptitude Test (SAT), given to college-bound students. Skinner himself graduated in 1994 with a strong 3.6 grade point average, but the quiet, humble man calls those "decent grades, not great grades. . . . But I had to work at it," he adds, noting that his older sister, Pamela, breezed through Temple with lots of As and little study a few years before Brian arrived.

The Skinner family was well respected in Temple. Brian's parents, James and Gladys, worked at the local hospital, where his dad was on the support staff in the urology department and his mom was a dietician. In addition, the family was active in a growing, vibrant church in town, Temple Bible Church.

"My parents were known in the community for their character, for their Christian beliefs. I was one of the first babies in the church nursery at our church when it was just beginning. It began with maybe 100 people, but it's grown to more than 3,000 people now. It is awesome how God works and how the church has grown. A lot of people didn't know about the church when it was small and on the other side of town."

The Skinners also used to be in another part of town. "When I was little, we lived on the east side of town. There were drugs and gangs. The fact that I experienced that has had some effect on me, but my parents kept me away from getting involved in those things. Eventually, we moved to a place that had lots of kids but didn't have those influences that I could have gotten mixed up in.

"I look at it, and I think God put His hands around me and my whole family by getting us away from that and getting us to a better place. Only the Lord knows where I would be if I had gotten caught up in that. I can look at a lot of my friends now who were there. A lot of them are either dealing drugs or dead."

Besides his parent's strong influence, the other aspect of Brian's life that kept him out of trouble was his faith. He trusted Jesus as Savior when he was just five years old. His mom had told him the plan of salvation, he attended Awana, and he even sat quietly and listened as his mom taught Bible studies for other women. But it took a bump on the head to get his attention. He was playing under the kitchen table when he raised up and banged his head against the table.

"As soon as I hit my head, I prayed to ask Jesus to save me." The bump may not have led to Brian's trusting Christ, but it has surely helped him remember the event.

That's as dramatic as Brian Skinner's testimony can get, he says. "My testimony is not as exciting as everyone else's. I wasn't into drugs [and] somebody came and shared the gospel with me. . . . I am grateful that I didn't have to go through those things and experience all that heartache and pain."

During his senior season, Brian began to think about another serious thing: college basketball. He was a Christian and a sought-after high school basketball player unsure where to take his basketball skills. A pact he made with a high school buddy helped him know which way to turn.

Roger, a teammate on the Temple Wildcats basketball team, was a lot like Brian "both on and off the court," though "he used to go out a little more than I did," Brian notes. As they talked about college, they discussed how good it would be to play at the same school. As the school year continued and they looked over the possibilities, they decided to make their campus visits together.

When it came time to visit Baylor University, they decided to talk with a former Temple student, Gerard Banks, who was already at Baylor. They bombarded him with questions about the school, and they liked what they heard.

"We went on what we felt in our hearts. Roger said that he felt God wanted him to go to Baylor. I wasn't ready to say that. I prayed about it for two or three days before I finally announced that I was going to Baylor too."

Roger liked Baylor being "a Christian organization . . . although it's not what you call a stereotypical Christian school. Plus, it was close to home. My parents could come to see my games, which was important. It had the characteristics I was looking for. Why would I go 3,000 miles away to a different school that offered the same things Baylor offered?"

At Baylor, Skinner established himself as a defensive force in the Big 12 Conference with his shot-blocking ability. In each of his four years with the Bears, he set a new record for blocked shots, eventually tallying 346 blocks, an average of 3.4 blocks per game.

So besides being big, what else can turn a person into a human vacuum cleaner on defense? According to Skinner, it's both an acquired skill and an instinctive one. "You have to learn it," he says. "You have to get the right timing. You have to know what to look for—what players do and what their characteristics are. It's really anticipation and guessing what the shooter is going to do. It's being able to adjust and make the quick decisions." Skinner was given the size, the timing, and the intrinsic skills. The observation and the anticipation he's had to improve on and learn as he listened to coaches who instructed him in the fine points of shot blocking.

But Skinner was more than just a defensive bear. He shot over 50 percent all four years, including an outstanding 60 percent from the field during his sophomore season. For his career, he averaged 57.5 percent, as he scored 1,702 points for a per game average of 16.5 points.

Playing for Harry Miller at Baylor, Skinner had many out-standing individual moments. One took place during a rematch against Louisiana State University during his junior year. Earlier, the Bears had traveled to Baton Rouge, where the LSU Tigers mauled the Bears by 30 points. The Tigers were ranked 25th in the country, so it was not a big surprise that they had defeated Baylor, but to lose by that much was embarrassing.

"We played horrible. We played bad. We didn't play like we should have." So the team went to work to get ready for the rematch, which was coming in a few days at home.

"The next time we played them, we won by one point in overtime. It showed how resilient we were in terms of working hard those four days. We knew what we had to do to prepare. It wasn't just a game; it was a redemption. We could make up for that loss somewhat by making the next game a win instead of a loss. I had 31 points and 13 rebounds. That was my biggest highlight because they had beat us by so much the week before."

Two major collegiate highlights for Brian Skinner occurred outside a Bear uniform. He wore the colors of the Stars and Stripes during two U.S. world competitions. After Skinner's sophomore year, he was a member of the USA Select team chosen to take on the 1996 Olympic Dream Team, made up of Grant Hill, Karl Malone, Shaquille O'Neal, Reggie Miller, David Robinson, and other future Hall of Famers. In a halftime shocker, Skinner and his teammates, including Tim Duncan and Brevin Knight, led the NBA stars by 17 points, 59–42. Could the kids beat the old pros? Well, not quite. The Dream Team put the pedal to the medal in the second half and defeated the challengers 96–90. Yet for Skinner and the others, it was a major thrill to nearly upset a team no one thought anyone in the world could beat.

Later that year, Skinner and the U.S. twenty-two-and-under World Championship qualifying team won the gold medal in the World Championships. It was a good warm-up for the international competition the following summer. In 1997 he was one of the top players selected to compete in the World University Games. Skinner was joined on this team by Bryce Drew of Valparaiso, Scott Padgett of Kentucky, Bonzi Wells of Ball State, and 5-foot-7 spark plug Earl Boykins of Eastern Michigan.

The team, coached by an all-Christian staff of head coach Jim Molinari of Bradley and assistants Dave Bliss of New Mexico and Ritchie McKay, then of Portland State, went to Italy and swept the competition, winning all six games and coming home with the gold medal. Skinner led the team with a .679 shooting percentage and 16 blocked shots. He averaged 7.2 rebounds during the tournament. Just as in college, his defense and his sharpshooting were his strong points as he helped lead the USA to the gold.

After Skinner's senior year at Baylor, during which he capped his career with an 18-points-per-game average, there was nothing to do but wait to see if his outstanding stats with the Bears and his impressive international showings had earned him the opportunity to take his game to the next level. Skinner watched on TV the 1998 NBA draft, originating from Vancouver. The L.A. Clippers, taking advantage of two selections in the first round, used their second pick to select Skinner, the twenty-second player chosen.

"From what they told me, the Clippers didn't know I was going to still be there. It was a quick decision they made when they saw I was still there."

Of course, their first choice, Michael Olowokandi from Pacific, made the biggest news, but you don't have to listen to Brian Skinner long before you know that the Clippers landed a special person in the kid from Temple.

"I was thankful that I was going to go from Waco, Texas, to Los Angeles, California. That was the last place I thought I would be drafted by. A lot of people who make it to the NBA take it for granted. They're like, "'I'm supposed to make it.' But statistics say a low percentage of players get to the NBA. So, I thank God for this opportunity."

As Skinner embarked on his NBA career—his opportunity—he had some extra time to think about what he would face. He was one of the unfortunate draftees who happened to come into the league at the time it was struggling to take care of some messy business matters. The ensuing lockout left the youngsters just coming in the league at a disadvantage. For one thing, they were not allowed to sign contracts—meaning they would have to go from their June draft date through the first part of February without a paycheck.

For another, they couldn't work out with the team under the watchful eye of their coach. Going to the YMCA and working out with the lunchtime accountants and lawyers just wasn't going to get the rookies ready for prime time.

Yet, although he may have faced those difficulties, Skinner knew what he had to do to get ready for the big switch from the Big 12 to the Big Show. He knew that he would be facing a huge adjustment period. "It's a totally different game than what college is. It's an adjustment. If you think it's just like college, it's not.

"There's more isolation, times when you have to basically guard your player all by yourself," notes Skinner. "In college, you can hang in the paint and not necessarily have to move. Everything's so much different in the pros. Even with wide open shots. If you get one, you'd better not miss it. Those are free opportunities and those are things that can make things a little easier. But you'd better hit the open shots and do the things you are supposed to do.

"Another thing is that in the pros, you're not going to have to do a wide variety of different things. You can't be the whole team. You have to find two or three things that you do exceptionally well, and you go with those things.

"You have to specialize. Look at a player like Dennis Rodman. He has no offensive game, but he specializes in defense and rebounding. People who spend the most time in the league find out where their niche is on the team and they utilize.

"So I'm trying to find out my niche. Am I going to be a rebounder or a shot blocker? I think the players that do figure it out and play within themselves play longer."

One of the initial battles Skinner faced when his initial season started was trying to find a place among the trees in Los Angeles: 7-foot-3 Keith Closs, 7-foot-2 Stojko Vrankovic, 6-foot-11 Lorenzen Wright, and 7-foot Olowokandi all fought for spots on the 1999 Clippers team.

"They're known for drafting a lot of forwards," Brian says in a tremendous understatement. For him to make a spot in the NBA among such tall timber, Skinner knew what he had to do. "They're not going to *give* you a spot. It's a competitive field. It's going to be a knock-down, drag-out kind of thing. If you want to start and if you want some playing time, you have to prove yourself game in and game out. You can't be lackadaisical.

"It's like being a freshman in college again, where I had to learn to give 100 percent every time out. I didn't know what to expect then, but now I do. I'm more prepared and more mature. I know what is expected of me."

As a first-round pick on a team that is hungry for a winner, and as a forward complement to Olowokandi's big-man game in the middle, Brian Skinner found himself in a good spot as his NBA career started. Though injuries slowed his progress in his first NBA season (arthroscopic surgery on his left knee kept him sidelined almost a month in the lockout-shortened season), once he got back on the floor, he did fine. His best success was against San Antonio, the team that ended the season with the best record. He averaged 6.7 points and 3 rebounds against the Spurs, proving that he indeed belongs in the NBA. And he seemed ready to pay back the Clippers for their faith in him, with strong, aggressive play.

"At Baylor, they were paying for my education. In the NBA, I'm paid to perform. When I get paid the money, I need to do whatever it takes to help the team. If that means playing aggressive, then I have to do that. I won't cross boundaries that would make people question whether I was a Christian or not. But I will play hard for the team. It's a matter of integrity. The needs of the many outweigh the needs of a few."

The NBA needs more people like Brian Skinner. People with quiet strength.

Q & A WITH BRIAN SKINNER

Q: *When life gets frustrating, what do you do to stay on track?*
Brian: I like to pray and stay close to God. I've been pretty much an independent person growing up. So I rely on the idea

that God and I can face anything. Sometimes, though, it's good to have some flesh there to depend on. That's when my parents and my sister help me.

Q: *How did having an older sister help you as you were growing up?*
Brian: Pamela is five years older than me. She played basketball at Concordia Lutheran College. She was really respected at Temple High School, so I didn't get messed with a lot in high school because of her. I used to play volleyball with her, and when she was on the team, I used to be the line judge. We played a lot of one-on-one basketball.

Q: *What do you like to do to stay strong spiritually?*
Brian: For some reason, I'm fascinated with the Psalms. I normally have my devotions in the morning, and I read the Psalms. It's not always easy to have [devotions]; sometimes I get bogged down with stuff and put it off. But that's like saying, "I'm not going to eat anything or drink anything the rest of the day." That's my sustenance for the day. I need that every day in terms of praying and staying in the Word and staying close to God. I've found that when I don't stay in the Word one or two days because I had something really important I had to take care of, it hurt me.

Also, my mom tends to put books in my car. I have no idea how she gets in there, but she'll leave documents and books from different Christian writers that apply to what I need to hear. I don't know how she knows what I need, but she does.

Q: *Do you think people can tell you are a Christian by how you play basketball?*
Brian: I don't think you can tell someone by the way they play; I think it's in how you carry yourself on and off the court. It also has a lot to do with whether or not they know you. You see a person one or two times; you can't get the idea of whether they are a Christian. You have to see them a couple of times, see how they act, see what they do, how they carry themselves. When I'm playing on the court, I'm aggressive. I play

hard; I play to win. I do whatever it takes to win.

With the cursing or all the gesturing and showing off, then that's where your Christian faith comes into play. You have to have self-control when you're out there.

NBA ROAD

1998: Selected by the Los Angeles Clippers as the 22nd player in the NBA draft

THE SKINNER FILE

Collegiate Record

College: Baylor University

Season	Team	G	FGM	FGA	Pct.	FTM	FTA	Pct.	Reb.	Ast.	Points	Avg.
94–95	Bay	18	98	164	.598	40	95	.421	147	9	236	13.1
95–96	Bay	27	187	311	.601	101	163	.620	250	16	475	17.6
96–97	Bay	30	196	349	.562	92	172	.535	253	26	484	16.1
97–98	Bay	28	192	347	.553	123	208	.591	265	15	507	18.1
Totals		**103**	**673**	**1171**	**.575**	**356**	**638**	**.558**	**915**	**66**	**1702**	**16.5**

NBA Season (Regular Season)

Season	Team	G	FGM	FGA	Pct.	FTM	FTA	Pct.	Reb.	Ast.	Points	Avg.
1999	LAC	21	33	71	.465	20	33	.606	53	0	86	4.1

Bryant Stith
The Virginian

VITAL STATISTICS

Bryant Lamonica Stith
Born: December 12, 1970, in Emporia, Virginia
6 feet 5, 190 pounds
College: University of Virginia
Position: Guard
Family: Wife, Barbara; sons, Brandan and Broderick; daughter,
  Bria

CAREER HONORS

- Became the 18th leading scorer in Nuggets' history (1998)
- Set the Nugget's rookie record for free-throw percentage (.832, 1992–93)
- Selected MVP of National Invitational Tournament (1992)
- Named to the first team All-ACC three straight years (1990–92)

NOT-SO-VITAL STUFF

- His favorite athlete is Julius Erving
- Bryant's middle name is Lamonica; he is named after the former Oakland Raiders quarterback Daryle Lamonica
- His bachelor of arts degree is in sociology and history

FAVORITE VERSE

"Do not conform any longer to the pattern of this world, but be transformed by the renewing of your mind. Then you will be able to test and approve what God's will is—his good, pleasing and perfect will" (Romans 12:2).

Bryant Stith

If Bryant Stith had been of basketball age back in the good old days of the American Basketball Association—those days of the red, white, and blue basketball, the high flying Julius Erving, and the original three-point line—he would have been a natural choice to be the star of the Virginia Squires. He was a high-scoring shooter coming out of college, a perfect fit in a league where scoring was everything. But most of all he would have been able to play in the state where he grew up, made a name for himself in high school, and stayed close by to star at the University of Virginia.

Oh, and one more thing. He might have had a chance to play with his all-time favorite basketball player, Julius Erving. It was in the ABA that Dr. J. would make his first mark in pro basketball—signing with the Virginia Squires just four months after Bryant Stith was born.

But, of course, by the time Bryant was ready to launch his pro career, the ABA was a dim memory; Dr. J. had long since moved to the NBA, won a championship, and retired; and some of the ABA teams had become a part of the NBA. One of those teams was the Denver Nuggets, the team on which Bryant Stith now plays.

Yet Virginia couldn't have been a better basketball home for Bryant. After all, the state known for its history was where he made history during his first twenty-one years.

From Bryant's birth in Emporia, Virginia, it seemed clear that sports would play an important part in his life. His Dad had been a basketball player during his youth. And the bouncing baby boy, born during the 1970 NFL season, received the somewhat unusual middle name of "Lamonica." It seems that Bryant's dad was an Oakland Raiders' fan, and especially of All-Pro quarterback Daryle Lamonica.

Indeed, the name may have made a difference. "My first love was football," confesses the NBA veteran. He began playing football at age seven in the "midget program" and loved the sport, playing hoops only occasionally. "Basketball was something I did on the side," he says, as if it were a part-time job at McDonald's. And to keep things as they should be, Bryant Lamonica was indeed a quarterback in football.

But then that mysterious event that all young boys wait impatiently for finally happened. Bryant grew. "Between my seventh and eighth grade years," he says, "I happened to grow five inches in the summer. That changed the complexion of my life. I was now the tallest kid, so I played basketball."

For the folks at Freeman Brunswick High School, that was good news indeed. When Bryant finally arrived in the ninth grade, he was ready to make his mark in roundball, having given up on the fall sport. He played varsity basketball all four years. His team played for the state championship three of those years.

While Byrant's dad, a truck driver, was influencing him to be athletically remarkable, his mother had other ideas. She was a world geography and history teacher at a rival high school, and she left no question in Bryant's mind that academics were important. "I grew up reciting the fifty states and capitals," he says, probably exaggerating only slightly.

The combined efforts of his parents bore some incredible fruit. Not only did Bryant establish himself as a basketball star coveted by such hoops giants as Duke, Georgia Tech, Virginia, and Villanova, but he also excelled in the classroom. By the time the dust settled on his high school basketball career, his team had won back-to-back Class AA state titles, and he had obtained a remarkable award as well for his academic work: he was named valedictorian of his senior class. He had the highest grades among the graduates, which was nice. He also had to give the valedictory address, which Bryant thought was not so nice. "I dreaded it," he still recalls. "But it was something I'll cherish for the rest of my life. It went great. I still have the tape, and we watch it occasionally to reflect."

There was still so much more to Bryant's young life than sports and getting good grades. There was also growing up in a community where, as he puts it, "I had ten mothers and twenty-five fathers." In other words, it was a close-knit community where everyone watched out for everyone else. He describes Freeman as "a very rural, very spiritual community. It's an area where you know everyone and you are welcomed in everyone's household. At any point in time, if anybody sees you getting out of line, they have the discretion to go ahead and correct you."

When he was just a child, Bryant trusted Jesus Christ as his Savior, and he feels that the community of Christians among whom he grew up helped him to maintain the right kind of lifestyle. "They helped you want to conduct yourself in a manner that is pleasing to the Lord."

And there's one more thing Freeman did for Bryant. It helped introduce him to his future wife, Barbara. The two were high school sweethearts. "I went back to my roots and got my first love," he says. It's no wonder that Bryant Stith loves Virginia. Virginia, he found out, is indeed for lovers.

Bryant and Barbara were married in 1994, after his second season in the NBA. They have three children: Brandan, Broderick, and Bria.

With Freeman Brunswick High's phenomenal record, Bryant caught recruiters' eyes as a high school senior. Several universities contacted him, but "it came down to choosing between Virginia and Duke," Bryant reports. "I felt that I had a better opportunity to play as a freshman and develop my skills while I was on the court at Virginia. That was the deciding factor."

Bryant burst on the scene at Charlottesville in his freshman year, averaging more than 15 points a game and being named the Atlantic Coast Conference Rookie of the Year. He went on to be named to the All-ACC team three times, average 19 points a game for his career, and finish as the Cavaliers' all-time leading scorer, with 2,516 points. It was a remarkable career.

When Stith looks back on those days at Virginia, three significant events related to basketball stand out. The first two might be expected. He appreciates being able to set the all-time scoring record as a Cavalier. And he considers the university's retiring his uniform special too.

But his top collegiate honor involves playing against a future teammate. Stith was voted the Most Valuable Player of the National Invitational Tournament his senior year. In the final game of the 1992 tournament, played at Madison Square Garden in the Big Apple, Stith led the Cavs to an 81–76 victory over LaPhonso Ellis and the Notre Dame Fighting Irish in overtime.

Bryant had admired LaPhonso for a long time; he had first become aware of him when they were both in high school. "I remember getting the magazine *Hoop Scoop* when I was in high school and seeing an article on sensational sophomores. LaPhonso was one of those players. That's the first time I had ever seen his name. I was very conscious of who was in my class and how they ranked and rated compared to me."

Then, in 1992 when the Cavs and the Irish met in New York, they met for the first time. "That's when we hit it off. We were staying at the same hotel, and we had a chance to spend some time together. We talked about predraft camps, and our friendship developed."

Little did they know that when the draft would roll around that summer, they would both be taken in the first round by the Denver Nuggets. They remained teammates for six years, until Ellis signed as a free agent with the Atlanta Hawks.

A couple of other important things happened to Stith while he was in college—events that aren't in any record books but have changed his life nonetheless. One relates to his understanding of his basketball future. The other relates to his faith.

As good as Bryant Stith was coming out of high school and playing for Virginia, he was not aware that he was a potential NBA player as he made his way through the first couple of years of college basketball. That would change because of his selection to the USA Basketball team after his sophomore year.

"That was when the college players represented the U.S. in the Goodwill Games and the World Championships. We were the last college team to play," he explains, making it sound a bit like the good old days. "When the president of USA Basketball addressed all of us who had made the final roster, he told us that every one of us would probably be making a million dollars for some NBA team some day. That's when it hit me like a ton of bricks that I really had a chance to advance to the next level."

Before Stith arrived for the tournament, the idea of playing professional basketball "was the farthest thing from my mind. . . . Coming from rural Virginia, sometimes you have a tendency to let your dreams be out of your reach. The USA Basketball situation helped me realize that it might become a reality."

The other important event that affected Stith during college was a renewed spiritual interest. Although he had put his faith in Christ when he was young, he realized during his senior year that he was not progressing. "After you come to Christ," he says, "it's a developmental process each and every day. I began to start growing in my senior year. I began to take steps forward and began to get into the Word and walk worthy of Christ.

"My best friend in college was Anthony Oliver. His dad was a minister. We were roommates and we had a fantastic relationship. We kept each other in line, and we always bounced ideas off each other."

They continue to maintain that close accountability relationship today.

When Stith and Ellis reunited at Denver after the Nuggets drafted both of them, Stith found that they, too, would share a similar bond as he had with Anthony. They both were growing Christians, and they both became active in the team chapel services organized by team chaplain Bo Mitchell.

For Stith, it was akin to having the brother he never had.

"We had so much in common it was uncanny," says Stith. "It was almost like he was my brother who was removed from my family. We basically shared the same interests and we shared the same tastes. It was easy for us to develop a type of camaraderie that is uncommon in the NBA."

They would certainly need each other as friends as the years passed, for what had begun as such a promising venture in Denver fell apart in many ways for both players and for the franchise.

His ability to score was something the Nuggets needed, since the team finished third to last in scoring in the NBA in 1991–92. Bryant quickly served notice that he was one of the answers the team needed. In his first game, the Virginian rookie poured in 20 points, grabbed 6 rebounds, and picked up 4 steals. He lead the Nuggets to a 125–121 double-overtime victory against the San Antonio Spurs. Six games later, he was in the starting lineup for the Nuggets. It was his first NBA start, and it was against Isaiah Thomas, Joe Dumars, and the Detroit Pistons.

Early in the game, disaster struck. Bryant broke his right foot. Talk about getting a career off on the wrong foot!

"I knew I could play at this level," he says now about his beginning days in the NBA, when injuries would sideline the talented rookie. "I had never been seriously injured before. The most significant injury I had was an ankle strain. To have broken my foot the night I was inserted into the starting lineup—it almost shattered my little world.

"That's when I got refocused and tried to understand that everything is revealed through God's ultimate plan. I just have to play it out."

That first season, after sitting out 32 games with the cracked bone in his foot, he came back and played in 32 more games. His stats were looking good—9 points a game and a .832 free-throw percentage. Then, on April 4, the Minnesota Timberwolves came to town. There were just 10 games left in a season; that left the Nuggets in the middle of the Midwest Division, hoping for the play-offs. That night, Bryant broke his right hand. That ended his rookie season.

For the next three years, Stith played injury-free. In both 1994 and 1995, the Nuggets, who many thought were a team on the rise, made the playoffs. In 1994, especially, Denver made the basketball world notice them when they knocked off the highly favored Seattle Sonics in the first round of the playoffs. During that season, Stith tied Dikembe Mutombo for team lead in minutes played and was fourth on the team in scoring. In one game, against the Spurs, he scored a career-high 33 points.

Named captain of the Nuggets in 1995, Stith extended his string of consecutive starts to 138 games until he was scratched from the starting lineup on February 14, 1995. Again the Nuggets made the playoffs, and Stith averaged 16 points a game in the first round, but Denver fell to San Antonio in three games. His rise to stardom continued in 1996 and 1997, as each year he increased his scoring average (almost 15 points during the 1997 season).

But then came the most frustrating year of his career. It was, of course, also the worst year in the Nuggets' history, and having Stith unavailable much of the season didn't help. First, on November 14, 1997, he was placed on the injured list with tendintis. A subsequent MRI showed that he had a bone spur in his left foot, and that required surgery. In all, Stith played just 31 games for the Nuggets and averaged just 7 points a game, his career low.

Then came the lockout. Some reports coming out of Denver said Stith was thinking of hanging up his shoes for the last time.

"It was becoming very frustrating battling injuries every season," he admits. "I had made a statement to my wife and to my family that at the end of this contract, this may be it. Combined with the injuries, the team was spiraling downward. It was taking a toll on my mentality. It was affecting my attitude off the court.

"You can't let that change your life, especially when you have a wife and three kids. You always have to remain strong. You are the source of strength in your household, and if your family sees you weakened and always saddened by your circumstances, then it's time to look for a change."

When it's time for Bryant Stith to reflect on something as important as his career, he knows just where to go. He goes back home to Virginia. Indeed, every summer following the NBA season, he returns to his roots.

"I retreat to Virginia. I have some strong support systems there. My family and my friends, they constantly pump Scriptures into my spirit. That enables me to rejuvenate my spirit and push forward. Also, during the off-season, there is an almost unspoken rule in our family. We take time out to worship the Lord weekly. That involves going to church and revivals."

After being rejuvenated in that way and after looking at what the Nuggets had done to revitalize their team—they hired a new coach, Mike D'Antoni, and had signed Antonio McDyess—Stith felt that things were on the upswing and he wanted to be a part of it. So he signed on with the Nuggets for another year. "This is a fresh start and I hope a new beginning for my career," he said before the 1999 season.

Of course, that was before LaPhonso Ellis left for Atlanta.

"That was very difficult," Bryant says. And he wasn't really available to help LaPhonso make the decision. "It was tough because we were in training camp when he was trying to make that decision. As a friend, I wanted to respect his privacy so he and Jennifer could make a very important decision."

So, with Ellis gone, Stith faced the frantic and crazy 1999 season. The season had its ups and downs, just as his career has. One of the ups was scoring 23 points against the Phoenix Suns. One of the downs was continuing injuries that cut into his playing time and limited his point production to another subpar year.

For Stith, it was time to recall a principle that has buoyed him throughout his career. "For those who love the Lord," he often reminds himself, "all things seem to work out for the good."

Far from home, Stith has learned to depend on the lessons he learned growing up in Freeman, Virginia. He has continued to trust that what happens to him as a basketball player is part of "God's ultimate plan," as he calls it. And he competes at the highest level in basketball, knowing that he can always go home again.

"Retreating to Virginia is very therapeutic for me. There, I'm around people who appreciate me for who I am and not just because I'm a basketball player. In 1998, when we had such a sour season, it got especially [hard]. Everybody was taking potshots at us, and we were the butts of everyone's jokes. Going home allows me to get away from that and enjoy life outside of basketball."

John Denver called West Virginia "almost heaven." It seems that Bryant Stith would suggest that an earthbound heaven for him is to the east of that state. He's a true Virginian who, though he may not play basketball there anymore, loves to go home.

And isn't that what everyone wishes for?

Q & A WITH BRYANT STITH

Q: *How do you stay strong spiritually during the season?*
Bryant: During the season, sometimes our schedule doesn't permit me to make it to church on Sunday, so I'm constantly studying the Word of God and trying to get as many of His Scriptures into my spirit. When you are put into a situation where you are squeezed, whatever is in you will come out. Therefore, you try to build your spirit up with the Word of God so when you are put into a difficult situation, you'll be able to handle it with loving-kindness.

Q: *How do you minister to others off the court?*
Bryant: In my everyday conversations with people, I try to be uplifting and I try to encourage them constantly. We are all shepherds, and we want to try to bring as many people into the fold as we can. It's very difficult at times with the family and trying to be a very productive NBA player to fit a ministry into your schedule. I have a lot of friends who are in ministry, and I go and speak to them on occasion; it's nothing that I do regularly.

Q: *You are one of the best free-throw shooters in the NBA. What's the secret to good shooting?*

Bryant: I think my shooting is something I have developed over the years. It's basically repetition. I pattern myself after some of the better shooters in the league. I have played with two of the best shooters in the game, Dale Ellis and Mahmoud Abdul-Rauf. They took me under their wings and showed me that in order to become a good free-throw shooter and a good shooter in general, it just comes down to hours and hours of practice. In the off-season, I usually shoot 100 free throws and 300 jumpers a day.

Q: *How does your faith show through when you are on the court?*

Bryant: One of the things at an early age that my mother and father taught me was humility. Especially when I was playing in high school when I was the best player on the court. They told me that you could always get more praise for your conduct and the way you handled yourself if you always encourage the other person and always try never to highlight your performance. Keep a calm demeanor out there on the basketball floor. That is something I've carried with me through the University of Virginia and here with the Denver Nuggets. And I think that serves as a testimony.

NBA ROAD

1992: Selected by the Denver Nuggets in the first round of the draft

THE STITH FILE

Collegiate Record
College: University of Virginia

Season	Team	G	FGM	FGA	Pct.	FTM	FTA	Pct.	Reb.	Ast.	Points	Avg.
88–89	VA	33	181	330	.548	150	195	.769	216	50	513	15.5
89–90	VA	32	217	451	.481	192	247	.777	221	53	666	20.8
90–91	VA	33	228	484	.471	159	201	.791	203	41	653	19.8
91–92	VA	33	230	509	.452	189	232	.815	219	72	684	20.7
Totals		**131**	**856**	**1774**	**.483**	**690**	**875**	**.789**	**859**	**216**	**2516**	**19.2**

Three-point field goals: 1988–89: 1-1 (1.000); 1989–90: 40-102 (.392); 1990–91: 38-125 (.304); 1991–92: 35-95 (.368). **Totals:** 114-323 (.353).

NBA Record (Regular Season)

Season	Team	G	FGM	FGA	Pct.	FTM	FTA	Pct.	Reb.	Ast.	Points	Avg.
92–93	DEN	39	124	278	.446	99	119	.832	124	49	347	8.9
93–94	DEN	82	365	811	.450	291	351	.829	349	199	1023	12.5
94–95	DEN	81	312	661	.472	267	324	.824	268	153	911	11.2
95–96	DEN	82	379	911	.416	320	379	.844	400	241	1119	13.6
96–97	DEN	52	251	603	.416	202	234	.863	217	133	774	14.9
97–98	DEN	31	75	225	.333	75	86	.872	65	50	235	7.6
1999	DEN	46	114	290	.393	61	71	.859	106	83	320	7.0
Totals		**413**	**1620**	**3779**	**.429**	**1315**	**1564**	**.841**	**1530**	**907**	**4729**	**11.5**

Three-point field goals:1992–93: 0-4; 1993–94: 2-9 (.222); 1994–95: 20-68 (.294); 1995–96: 41-148 (.277); 1996–97: 70-182 (.385); 1997–98: 10-48 (.208); 1999: 31-106 (.292). **Totals:** 174-565 (.308).

Charlie Ward
The Transformer

VITAL STATISTICS

Charlie Ward, Jr.
Born: October 12, 1970, in Thomasville, Georgia
6 feet 2 inches, 190 pounds
College: Florida State University
Position: Guard
Family: Wife, Tonja

CAREER HONORS

- Coupled 14 points with 13 assists against the Chicago Bulls (1998)
- Recorded his 1,000th career assist during the 1999 season
- Played in every game in 1998
- Won the Heisman Trophy as the best collegiate football player (1993)
- Received the Sullivan Award as top amateur athlete (1993)

NOT-SO-VITAL STUFF

- Was drafted by both the Milwaukee Brewers and the New York Yankees
- His favorite vacation spot is St. Thomas
- Was the vice president of the student body at Florida State

FAVORITE VERSE

"I can do everything through him [Christ] who gives me strength" (Philippians 4:13).

Charlie Ward

Several years ago the toy industry came up with a concept that made a lot of people a ton of money and provided boys and girls across the United States with bushels of happiness. The concept was to put together a toy that looked like one kind of object (a truck or a car, for instance) but could be changed into something totally different with a little manipulation by the youngster playing with it.

Transformers, they were called.

Charlie Ward would have been a great model for the hit toys.

His life has undergone a number of major transformations—changes from what he was to what he is or what he is becoming. And in some cases, those transformations are as remarkable as changing a truck into a man with a few turns and twists.

The change for which Charlie Ward is most noted by sports fans is the transformation that took place in his life after a stellar senior year as quarterback at Florida State University. The All-American quarterback from Thomasville, Georgia, stood before the New York Downtown Athletic Club in December 1993, holding in his hand the Heisman Trophy. He had just been named the very best college football player in the United States.

What usually happens about four months later is that the winner of the Heisman is honored once more by being selected as a first-round draft pick by a pro football team that thinks he can do for them on Sundays what he had done for his college team on Saturdays. But in one of the most shocking and surprising nonevents in pro football draft history, each and every NFL team passed on the opportunity to take a quarterback who had led his team to a national championship. They opted not to choose a young man who was a leader at his school, who was exemplary in his behavior, and who had passed for more than 3,000 yards and 27 touchdowns in his senior year for the Seminoles. They chose not to pick a person who valued the team accomplishment of winning the national title more than he did the individual thrill of receiving one of sport's most coveted awards.

"The national championship was a greater accomplishment because it was a team effort," he says. "We all played a part in it. You can't do it alone." That altruistic attitude aside, Ward was in reality ignored by some people who could have used his skills.

When the last draft pick had been called on that April day in 1994, the name Charlie Ward was still on the board. The Heisman Trophy winner had gone undrafted.

For most youngsters, that would have been the most devastating blow of their lives. For most college football stars, not being summoned to wear the logo of an NFL team would be crushing—the end of a dream, the death of a lifelong desire, the beginning of life without a sport to play.

But Ward was not one of those college gridiron stars whose all-consuming drive was to play in the NFL. Even during the time leading up to the draft, Ward's perceived lack of hunger for NFL action was one of the reasons some teams cited for not picking him.

When Ward went undrafted, he told an Associated Press writer simply, "The Lord is going to guide me in the right direction."

He later amplified that statement by saying, "I think it [not being selected] was a blessing. It gave me an opportunity to say, 'Hey, football may not be for me.' The Lord's blessed me with athletic ability, and He's given me the choice to play football or basketball. I chose basketball."

And so he became the Transformer, moving into professional basketball, becoming a steady point guard for the New York Knicks.

As he looks back now on his college days, Ward recalls not really putting much stock in his prospects of becoming a professional athlete—football *or* basketball—during his time at FSU.

"Up until my senior year," Charlie says, "I didn't think of either the NFL or the NBA. Until it came time for football to end, I really didn't have any aspirations of going anywhere. I was having so much fun I really didn't sit down and think about it. I was taking care of my education."

A college senior year couldn't have been much more fun than the one Charlie Ward had at Florida State. There was the little thing about leading the Seminoles to the national championship and winning the Heisman Trophy.

Then there was basketball, which he played alongside three other future NBA players, Sam Cassell, Doug Edwards, and Bob Sura. Ward was considered one of the top collegiate point guards in the country, despite missing nearly half of the last two seasons because of football. By the time he was through, Charlie was FSU's career leader in steals and ranked third in assists.

There were his classes, in which Charlie excelled, earning his bachelor of arts degree in therapeutic recreation with honors. In fact, by the time his final year rolled around, he had already finished his course work and was taking extra classes in his field.

And there was his success in student government, for which he was student body vice president.

He was living the dream senior year of college, so why would something as far away as a possible NFL career bother a young man who had the world right where he wanted it?

"I didn't really know what I was going to do," he says. "I was just preparing myself. I was getting my degree and doing what I had to do on the football field."

To most people, Ward's basketball career at Florida State appeared to be an afterthought. It was a strange combination—basketball and football. The more usual two-sport route is baseball and football, as demonstrated by Deion Sanders and John Elway (who once had a chance to play for the Baltimore Orioles). Or baseball and basketball, as with old-timers Dave DeBusschere and Chuck Connors or, more recently, Danny Ainge, with the Toronto Blue Jays and the Boston Celtics.

For Charlie, it could have been *three* sports. During high school, Charlie played football, basketball, and baseball. In fact, after his junior year of college, he was drafted by the Milwaukee Brewers. After his senior year, the New York Yankees used an 18th round pick to try to lure Charlie to the diamond.

Sports had always been a major part of Charlie's life. It came naturally, since his dad had been a fine athlete in his day, excelling for Florida A & M. Later, Charlie Sr. became a teacher and a coach at Thomasville Central High School, and Charlie was one of his student-athletes.

The Ward home was a nurturing place for Charlie and his six brothers and sisters. His mother, Willard, who was an elementary teacher, and Charlie Sr. instilled a strong work ethic in their brood. Once, when Charlie was in the third grade, he was struggling with his reading. His mother, who knew where he should have been academically, was afraid he might have a learning disability, that perhaps his mind couldn't collect the information it needed.

Then one day she heard Junior recalling for his dad an incredible amount of sports information from a football game he had been watching. She deduced correctly that Charlie was not slow mentally. He was just being lazy. Willard put a stop to that. From then on, she knew that if Junior wasn't doing well, it was because he wasn't trying.

"My parents have been the main leaders in my life," a grateful Charlie says now. "They've been there for me and my siblings. They've been leaders. Their actions showed us the way."

Ward would be a leader in two sports during his final year at Florida State. After the hype and the Heisman, Charlie moved over to the gym and suited up for hoops. In the previous season, Ward had helped lead the Seminoles to its first NCAA Elite Eight appearance. During his senior year, he was selected to play in the National Association of Basketball Coaches All-Star Game. His stellar play in that contest earned him the Most Valuable Player award.

That was all the scouts needed to see. Although the NFL scouts couldn't project him into an important role on their football teams, NBA scouts saw something they liked. In April, Ward was drafted by the New York Knicks as one of their guards of the future.

Even before Charlie suited up in a Knicks uniform he convinced the team that their pick had not been wasted. During the summer of 1994, Charlie played in the NBA summer league—a great seasoning time for new NBA players and others who needed to get used to the next step of competition. At the end, Ward was named the league's Most Valuable Player.

The transformation was complete. Ward had gone from football superstar to an up-and-coming leader for one of professional basketball's top franchises.

One of the great things about Charlie Ward is his willingness to listen and learn. That trait bode well for him in a sport in which he had much less experience than many of the other players in the league.

A testament to Ward's coachability is the fact that he credits former Knicks coach Pat Riley with helping him by not allowing him to play. Says Charlie, "Pat Riley helped me in a sense by not playing me in my rookie year, so I could get better first." When's the last time you heard an NBA player thank his coach for *not* playing him?

Indeed, Ward saw action in just ten games that first year with New York, scoring a miserly 16 points for the season. Yet that time of waiting and preparing served him well. For the next three seasons, with his playing time, scoring, steals, and rebounds increasing each year, Ward went from 62 games played in 1995–96 to playing in all of the Knicks games in 1997–98.

The 1997–98 year was a breakthrough season for Ward. Finally called on to lead the team, he often was the team spark plug. As a true playmaker, the point guard is not noted for his point totals. Yet he reached a career-high 19 points against Portland in March of 1998. A month later, against the Chicago Bulls, he recorded 14 assists to go along with 13 points. An indication of his newfound respect around the league was the fact that he was picked to participate in the AT&T Shootout at the 1998 All-Star Game. Ward finished fourth in the contest.

During those growing times, he received valuable tutelage as he learned the intricacies of NBA battle. His main tutor was teammate Derek Harper, and another was his coach, Jeff Van Gundy, who took over the team during the 1995–96 season.

"Derek Harper helped me as far as learning to play the game," Charlie says. Harper was Ward's teammate during Charlie's first three years in the league. From Harper, whom he sat next to in the locker room, Ward says he learned how to conduct himself as a professional off the court.

And of his coach, Ward says, "Jeff Van Gundy helped me with my skills."

The transformation from football star to basketball star has been exciting and unusual, but it's far from the most important transformation Ward has undergone in the past several years. The change that has made the biggest difference is spiritual.

The spiritual journey has been a lifelong one for Ward. The grandson of a minister and the third child in a family that was in church every Sunday, Charlie trusted Christ as a youngster. "When I was ten, I gave my life to Christ while attending church," he says.

At the time, he realized how tough it was for a kid to make such a choice. "That was a bold decision within itself," he recalls. "You always think about your friends and worry about what they're going to say. At that time, peer pressure is tough, and I really didn't have many friends. I was just trying to know what was going on."

After being baptized at age ten, Ward began the long road to spiritual maturity, something that he likes to call "a growing process."

As it is for many young people, spiritual growth was a bumpy road for Charlie.

One of the major bumps in the road came when he was in his first couple of years of high school—a physical difficulty he turned into a spiritual triumph. He suffered a knee injury that seemed at first to be a threat to any sports career he might have ahead of him. Today, he can look back on that injury in a positive way. "It helped me out a lot because if I wouldn't have had that, I might not have had my faith as strong as it is now. I thank the Lord for giving me that opportunity to seek Him more."

In fact, the injury helped in another way. It gave him direction for a science project he had to do that year. The project was titled "Knee Injuries." And who knows, perhaps that's one of the reasons he majored in therapeutic recreation at Florida State.

While in college, Charlie's growth as a Christian continued. He was involved in campus activities such as Fellowship of Christian Athletes, but he admits that he was not spiritually mature at the time. That became evident to one sportswriter who interviewed Charlie first in 1993, soon before he won his Heisman Trophy, then again in 1998. During the later interview, Charlie's answers and the extent to which he explored spiritual matters revealed a spiritual transformation.

In contrast, in the first interview, Charlie's answers were so short and lacking substance that the writer, after finishing the interview, began to wonder about his own skills as an interviewer. In fact, the writer, who had planned to run the story on Charlie as an interview, had so little information that he had to turn it into a feature article based mostly on research and very little on Charlie's comments. There was only enough spiritual content in Charlie's answers to include two or three short quotes about his faith. Now, five years later, he answers questions about his football and basketball careers with friendly, but somewhat short answers—but answers about his Christian life that are complete, thorough, and presented with enthusiasm.

That "growing process" that Ward says should accompany the Christian life was indeed in operation.

One of the most vital components of Charlie's transformation from run-of-the-mill believer in college to sold-out follower of Jesus now is the influence of his wife, Tonja. The two began dating when Charlie was a senior and she was in law school at the University of Miami, but they had been friends much longer. Tonja was the daughter of lifelong friends of Charlie's parents, Charlie and Willard. Tonja's dad had coached with Charlie's dad even before the two of them were born.

As they dated, many people didn't know who she was because she wasn't from the FSU campus. "People thought she was just someone who came on the scene trying to get the hype. She was like a friend the whole time." A friend, yes, but more than just a friend. "If it wasn't for a couple of other people we were dating in college, we probably would have gotten together sooner," Charlie admits. "But that wasn't God's plan for our lives. He put her in the right time and the right place. I thank God for Tonja."

A year after they began dating, Tonja and Charlie were engaged after he proposed to her as they were getting ready to go on a special date—a New York Knicks Christmas party hosted by Pat Riley. They were married the following summer, on August 26, 1995.

Together, they've grown spiritually, helping to continue that transformation that has turned Charlie into one of the top ministry-oriented players in the NBA. For Charlie and Tonja, spiritual growth is something they work on together. Each day they have a time of devotional reading together. They will read a Scripture and something from a book together and discuss it.

Sometimes those discussions last into the night. Once, he said, they came upon a question they didn't know the answer to, so they stayed up until past 2:00 A.M. reading the Bible, searching the truth.

Besides Tonja, Charlie has other spiritual counselors who challenge him to live a strong life of Christian discipleship. One of those people is Keith Johnson, chaplain for the Minnesota Vikings. Keith meets with Charlie regularly to keep him accountable spiritually.

Another of his key spiritual guides is Robert Waterman, who works with Charlie in his outreach endeavors. For instance, if Charlie is invited to a youth rally, he'll take Waterman with him to do the preaching. As an evangelist, Waterman has an ability to present the gospel. Ward draws them in, Waterman waters, and they wait for God's blessing.

"He's really challenged me," Charlie says. "He helps me to understand the Bible better."

This spiritual growth Charlie has experienced over the past several years has led him to still another transformation. Once an admittedly shy, reserved type, he has become an outspoken conveyor of the gospel. He does this in several ways.

One is through his basketball camps. Each summer, he conducts two camps in Erie, Pennsylvania, at the Family First Sports Park. Also, he has camps in his hometown in Georgia. "I'm trying to teach kids the Bible and how to study it. We put them in an environment they can enjoy. We have a lot of campers who welcome the idea of learning about God and the Bible." It works. During one of his camps in 1998, thirty young people trusted Jesus Christ as Savior.

Another outreach activity Charlie is trying to get off the ground was one that was hampered a bit in 1999 by the NBA lockout. Charlie's idea was to put together what he called a Hopefest each February in the city of the NBA All-Star Game. "We want to do this at every All-Star break because there is no outlet for the Christian people who want to come and be a part of something positive, instead of drinking and dancing for Satan."

Since the 1999 game was scheduled for Philadelphia, Ward pinpointed Camden, New Jersey, as the site of Hopefest 1999. The game was canceled by the shortened season; yet despite the lack of an NBA Weekend, the event took place as scheduled.

A third opportunity Ward enjoys is conducting youth rallies. This is when he involves his mentor, traveling evangelist Robert Waterman. Tonja is also involved, helping organize young people at their church to be involved with music and other activities.

The list of activities in which Charlie gives to others is long and impressive:

• Working as a Big Brother
• Creating a basketball camp for kids who have been physically or sexually abused

- Working with Nike in a program to provide basketball shoes for kids in Harlem
- Participating in Fellowship of Christian Athletes (FCA) activities
- Writing a book called *Winning by His Grace,* published in association with FCA

Charlie's goal now, it seems, is to transform others. It's part of the growing process that began in him when he was just a ten-year-old Little Leaguer back in Thomasville. And he recognizes how much he has grown, especially since those heady days of Heisman Trophy glory.

"It's been a time of tremendous growth, which is the way it should be," he says, thinking back over the years. "People have challenged me in my faith to do more than just settling for going to FCA, just settling for going to church.

"They've challenged me to study the Bible. In college, I read the Bible, but I still had things I was weak in.

"Tonja and I were reading in Romans 8 about life in the Spirit. Romans 7 talks about struggling with sin, how we can't do it through the flesh, because we don't have any confidence in the flesh. If you feed the flesh, it's going to take over the soul. If you feed the spirit, that's who you're going to be. If you feed the flesh more than you feed the spirit, you're in trouble.

"I'm just trying to challenge other people who may be where I was two or three years ago. I want to challenge them to take their life as Christians to another level."

There it is. Transformation. The Transformer is still at it.

Q & A WITH CHARLIE WARD

Q: *Why did you choose to attend Florida State University?*
Charlie: One of the reasons is because it's only thirty minutes from my hometown of Thomasville, Georgia. I was very close to my family, and if I had my option to go anywhere it was going to be close. It was also good because I knew they were going to play for the national championship every year. It was a good school for me.

Q: *Where is the Heisman Trophy, and what does it mean to you?*
Charlie: It is in the library in Thomasville, Georgia. The Heisman was great because it was something that was individual, something you can look at twenty years from now. However, it wasn't on my list of the things I had to do that year.

Q: *You have chosen Philippians 4:13 as your favorite verse. Why is Christ's strength in you, a strong athlete, important?*
Charlie: It's something that overcomes all obstacles. Whenever you feel like you don't have the strength to keep going, Christ can give you strength.

Q: *What kind of literature do you and Tonja use to enhance your spiritual growth?*
Charlie: We like *Our Daily Bread.* It has some really tough spiritual truths. I remember one article about 1 John about how we take things out of context sometimes. We have our favorite Bible verse, and we take it out of context. We make it say whatever we want it to say. Those little truths are very helpful.

Q: *What keeps you going during an especially frustrating time?*
Charlie: It definitely helps to have inner peace. When you understand that a time of trial is only a part of your life, it's not your whole life, then things don't bother you as much as they would if that was all that you do. It's always good to have Christ in your life first and foremost, because once you have Him first, everything else is something He's blessed you with, something extra.

Keep things prioritized and everything will be fine. But a lot of people get out of shape when things don't go their way. I'm not saying that I don't either, but we have to understand that God forgives us for our mistakes. We can't get to the point where it frustrates us to no end.

NBA ROAD

1994: Selected by the New York Knicks in the first round

THE WARD FILE

Collegiate Record
College: Florida State University

Season	Team	G	FGM	FGA	Pct.	FTM	FTA	Pct.	Reb.	Ast.	Points	Avg.
90–91	FSU	30	81	178	.455	62	87	.713	89	103	239	8.0
91–92	FSU	28	72	145	.497	35	66	.530	90	122	201	7.2
92–93	FSU	17	49	106	.462	18	27	.667	45	93	132	7.8
93–94	FSU	16	61	167	.365	25	40	.625	39	78	168	10.5
Totals		**91**	**263**	**596**	**.441**	**140**	**220**	**.636**	**263**	**396**	**740**	**8.1**

Three-point field goals: 1990–91: 15-48 (.313); 1991–92: 22-48 (.458); 1992–93: 16-50 (.320); 1993–94: 21-83 (.253). **Totals:** 74-229 (.323).

NBA Record (Regular Season)

Season	Team	G	FGM	FGA	Pct.	FTM	FTA	Pct.	Reb.	Ast.	Points	Avg.
94–95	NY	10	4	19	.211	7	10	.700	6	4	16	1.6
95–96	NY	62	87	218	.399	37	54	.685	102	132	244	3.9
96–97	NY	79	133	337	.395	95	125	.760	220	326	409	5.2
97–98	NY	82	235	516	.455	91	113	.805	274	466	642	7.8
1999	NY	50	135	334	.404	55	78	.705	170	270	378	7.6
Totals		**283**	**594**	**1424**	**.417**	**285**	**380**	**.750**	**644**	**1199**	**1689**	**6.0**

Three-point field goals: 1994–95: 1-1 (1.00); 1995–96: 33-99 (.333); 1996–97: 48-154 (.458); 1997–98: 81-215 (.377); 1999: 53-149 (.356). **Totals:** 216-627 (.344).